WRITERS AND THEIR WORK

ISOBEL ARMSTRONG
General Editor

GW00320434

THE MERCHANT
OF VENICE

Antony Sher as a terrifying Shylock, Royal Shakespeare Company, 1987.

WW

William Shakespeare

THE
MERCHANT
OF VENICE

Warren Chernaik

NORTHCOTE
BRITISH
COUNCIL

For Judith

© Copyright 2005 by Warren Chernaik

First published in 2005 by Northcote House Publishers Ltd, Horndon, Tavistock, Devon, PL19 9NQ, United Kingdom.
Tel: +44 (01822) 810066. Fax: +44 (01822) 810034.

British Library Cataloguing-in-Publication Data
A catalogue record for this book is available from the British Library

ISBN 0-7463-1074-9 hardcover
ISBN 0-7463-0995-3 paperback

Typeset by TW Typesetting, Plymouth, Devon
Printed and bound in the United Kingdom by
Athenaeum Press Ltd., Gateshead, Tyne & Wear

Contents

Acknowledgements

For help with illustrations and with research into the play's stage history, I would particularly want to thank librarians at the British Library, the Theatre Museum, the Shakespeare Centre Library, the National Portrait Gallery archive, the Victoria and Albert Museum picture library, and the University of London Library. For conversations about Shakespeare over the years, I would like to thank Bill Overton, James Shapiro, Ann Thompson, Bryan Cheyette, B. J. and Mary Sokol, Gordon McMullan, Richard Proudfoot, Kate McLuskie, John Peacock, and Jonathan Sawday. I owe a particular debt to Ruth Pitman, who invited me to participate in a seminar on *Merchant* at the British Association of Psychotherapists in November 2002, to my fellow panelists on that occasion, David Calder (who provided unusual insights into what it was like to play Shylock), Michael Billington, and Mary Twyman, and to Ann Thompson, for inviting me to give a version of Chapter 1 at the London Shakespeare Seminar. I am grateful to Isobel Armstrong for commissioning the book, and to Brian Hulme as publisher and Hilary Walford as a very efficient and helpful copy-editor. And I must express my gratitude to three directors of memorable productions of *Merchant*, Jonathan Miller, John Barton, and Trevor Nunn, and to Gerard Benson, who played Shylock to my Antonio in a play reading some years ago. My greatest debt, as always, is to my wife, Judith Chernaik, and to my students at the University of Southampton and Queen Mary, University of London.

List of Illustrations

Cover illustration and frontispiece: Antony Sher as Shylock, Royal Shakespeare Company, 1987, directed by Bill Alexander. Joe Cocks Studio collection, copyright Shakespeare Birthplace Trust. Shakespeare Centre Library, Stratford-upon-Avon.

Between pages 44–45

1 Henry Irving as Shylock, Lyceum, 1879. Ink drawing by Harry Furniss, National Portrait Gallery archive drawings collection.

2 Venetian street scene, *Merchant of Venice*, Act II, scene vi, Charles Kean production, Princess's theatre, 1858. By permission of the Shakespeare Centre Library, Stratford-upon-Avon.

3 Laurence Olivier as Shylock, Jeremy Brett as Bassanio, National Theatre, 1970, directed by Jonathan Miller. Photograph by Anthony Crickmay, Theatre Museum, copyright V&A Images.

4 Laurence Olivier as Shylock, National Theatre, 1970, directed by Jonathan Miller. Photograph by Anthony Crickmay, Theatre Museum, copyright V&A Images.

5 Patrick Stewart as Shylock, Avril Carson as Jessica, Royal Shakespeare Company, 1978, directed by John Barton. Joe Cocks Studio collection, copyright Shakespeare Birthplace Trust. Shakespeare Centre Library, Stratford-upon-Avon.

Note on the Text

All references to *The Merchant of Venice* are to the Arden edition, edited by John Russell Brown (London: Methuen, 1964). Quotations from other plays by Shakespeare are from the Arden editions of the individual plays, except for *Sir Thomas More*, quoted from *The Riverside Shakespeare*, ed. G. Blakemore Evans and J. J. M. Tobin, 2nd edn (Boston: Houghton Mifflin, 1997).

Introduction: The Problem of *The Merchant of Venice*

No play by Shakespeare is more problematical and subject to controversy than *The Merchant of Venice*. The play does not fit comfortably into any generic category. Uncertainty as to whether the play is a comedy, a tragedy, or some unstable mixture of the two has, as we shall see, been a recurrent element in the *Merchant*'s stage and critical history. In the puzzled words of Nicholas Rowe, in his 1709 edition of Shakespeare:

> Tho' we have seen that Play Receiv'd and Acted as a Comedy, and the Part of the *Jew* perform'd by an Excellent Comedian, yet I cannot but think it was design'd Tragically by the Author. There appears in it such a deadly Spirit of Revenge, such a savage Fierceness and Fellness, and such a bloody designation of Cruelty and Mischief, as cannot agree with either the Stile or Characters of Comedy.[1]

Northrop Frye, with wholly different critical assumptions, sees the play as liminal, testing the boundaries of genre, 'almost an experiment in coming as close as possible to upsetting the comic balance'.[2] The discordant elements in the play, mostly associated with the figure of Shylock, are not, as one would expect in a comedy, resolved into a final harmony, but remain unassimilated, irreconcilable, threatening to swamp the play and leave a bitter aftertaste.

What makes the play so controversial, more than anything else, is its alleged anti-Semitism. In his essay 'Shylock and the Idea of the Jew', Derek Cohen has characterized *The Merchant of Venice* as 'a profoundly and crudely anti-Semitic play',

1

arguing that attempts with 'critical sophistries . . . to exonerate Shakespeare' do not sufficiently take account of 'the fear and shame that Jewish audiences and readers have always felt from the moment of Shylock's entrance to his final exit'.[3] The dramatist Arnold Wesker accuses the play of 'iredeemable anti-semitism': 'The Jew in Shakespeare's play is meant to embody what he wishes to despise . . . The portrayal of Shylock offends by being a lie about the Jewish character . . . I'm unforgiving, unforgiving of the play's contribution to the world's astigmatic and murderous hatred of the Jew . . . It is a hateful, ignorant portrayal.'[4]

Both Wesker and Cohen see the play as pandering to anti-Semitic prejudice in its audience; indeed, Wesker has gone so far as to write an alternative version, *Shylock*, to counter the play's malign influence. On several occasions, memories of the Holocaust have prompted suggestions that proposed productions or televised broadcasts be withdrawn or the play removed from school syllabi:

> The authority of a great dramatist reinforces those people who are inclined toward anti-Semitism . . . I'm especially afraid of a television production: young people will see it, and they don't have the antibodies to resist the infection that Shakespeare so skillfully offers . . . And if we are in a period of increased anti-Semitism . . . then the showing of it at this time would seem to exacerbate these attitudes.[5]

The ideology of *The Merchant of Venice* is thus likely to generate feelings of unease in a modern audience. Its portrayal, in its most memorable figure, of a Jewish money-lender who is cruel, avaricious, consumed by bitterness and hatred, unrelenting in his pursuit of revenge against those he considers his enemies, can stir up shame and guilt in Jews and non-Jews alike, confronted in performance or in the printed text with this threatening embodiment of the Other. The motif of the pound of flesh, as James Shapiro has pointed out, can be seen as a variant of the blood-libel (the claim, found in Chaucer's 'Prioress's Tale' and elsewhere, of the ritual murder of Christian children by Jews) and as the symbolic equivalent of castration.[6] One curious aspect of the play's theatrical history has been how frequently productions have quietly excised

Shylock's lines 'I hate him for he is a Christian' and 'Cursed be my tribe if I forgive him' in Act I, presumably as too strong for the delicate sensibilities of theatre-goers.

Critics and directors have sought by a number of strategies to exorcize the demon of anti-Semitism in approaching *The Merchant of Venice*. One critical tradition, in which the most notable exponent is E. E. Stoll, has chosen to emphasize the ways in which Elizabethan ideological assumptions differ from those prevalent in later years: 'the hatred of Jews', Stoll argues, was widespread in Elizabethan England, so 'why should we refuse to recognize it in Shakespeare, who, more than any other poet, reflected the settled prejudices and passions of his race?'.[7] To Stoll, any attempt by later interpreters to view Shylock as a complex figure with tragic dimensions was a misinterpretation, violating the author's plain intention: to present in Shylock 'a comic villain', a 'ludicrous' figure conforming both to the conventions of the Elizabethan stage and to the 'popular detestation and ridicule' of Jews and usurers at this time.[8] A more theoretically sophisticated and less reductive attempt to situate *The Merchant of Venice* in the ideological assumptions of its time – 'what Shakespeare and contemporaries thought about Jews' – is Shapiro's carefully researched *Shakespeare and the Jews*.[9]

A different approach to the problem of anti-Semitism is to reinterpret the play in terms sympathetic to Shylock as a member of a persecuted society. The tradition probably originates with the celebrated performance of Edmund Kean at Drury Lane in 1814, which emphasized the character's 'family love and racial pride, both being subjected to suffering and pain'.[10] Hazlitt, commenting on the 'deep sense of justice' brought out in Kean's performance, writes in 1817:

> The constant apprehension of being burnt alive, plundered, banished, reviled, and trampled on, might be supposed to sour the most forbearing nature … The desire of revenge is almost inseparable from the sense of wrong, and we can hardly help sympathizing with the proud spirit, hid beneath his 'Jewish gaberdine', stung to madness by repeated undeserved provocations.[11]

A similar desire to see the events of the play from Shylock's point of view, treating him as 'wronged' and his enemies as 'hardly worthy to unloose the latchets of his shoes', animates the powerful defence of Shylock by the poet Heine:

> The Drama shows us neither Jew nor Christian exclusively, but oppressor and oppressed ... There is something that he prizes above money; satisfaction for a tortured heart ... There are things which he loves still more, among them his daughter 'Jessica, my girl' ... Debarred from public intercourse, outcast from Christian society, and thrust back upon a narrow domestic life, to the poor Jew there remains only devotion to his house, and this is manifested in him with the most touching intensity.[12]

The Romantic view of the play turns it into an attack on anti-Semitism. Though later, post-Holocaust interpretations rarely go as far as to see, with Heine, a 'breast that held in it all the martyrdom which, for eighteen centuries, had been borne by a whole tortured people',[13] many of the most acclaimed productions of the play have, as we shall see, been essentially philo-Semitic, focusing attention on the causes and consequences of anti-Semitism.

A dignified Shylock, deeply conscious of family ties and his position as a Jew in a hostile society, has been the central figure in three celebrated productions: Henry Irving's elaborately staged Victorian *Merchant* (first performed in 1879, with frequent revivals until 1905), the National Theatre production of 1970 directed by Jonathan Miller and starring Laurence Olivier, and the Trevor Nunn production of 1999, with Henry Goodman as Shylock, again at the National Theatre. The first two of these, though not the third, were characterized by significant cuts and a conscious attempt to tilt the balance of sympathies towards Shylock and away from the other characters in the play. Indeed, a recurrent tendency in both critical commentaries and productions has been a certain hostility towards the Venetians other than Shylock as essentially a worthless lot, shallow and materialistic: in Hazlitt's memorable phrase, 'he is honest in his vices; they are hypocrites in their virtues'.[14] In a play in which Shylock, the star role, appears in only five scenes, there is a strong temptation for directors and critics to rewrite Shakespeare's text as *Shylock: A Tragedy*, ignoring the counterpoint of juxtaposed Venetian and Belmont scenes throughout the play. No production I have seen has

4

followed Irving's example (in 1880 and afterwards) in leaving out Act V and making massive cuts in the other scenes in which Shylock does not appear,[15] but two productions of the 1980s, with famous actors in the lead role, seemed to me to distort the play almost beyond recognition, by treating the Belmont scenes as tedious interruptions of the main business.

In its dramatic structure, *The Merchant of Venice* resembles a number of Shakespeare comedies in contrasting two physical locations, each given symbolic significance. One of these, in Northrop Frye's terminology, is a 'green world', often associated with moonlight, dreams, the imagination set free, whereas the other is a severely restricted 'normal world' of fears, jealousies, and fears.[16] In *Merchant*, the two contrasted worlds are Venice and Belmont, in *As You Like It* the court of the usurping Duke and the Forest of Arden, in *A Midsummer Night's Dream* Athens and the fairies' magical wood (the American film *The Wizard of Oz* follows the same pattern, with Kansas in black and white, and Oz, the land over the rainbow, in resplendent technicolor). In each play, a number of characters leave the first world to enter the second and come under its influence, and then return, changed in some respects, to their point of origin. In *Merchant*, Bassanio makes the journey to Belmont, accompanied by Gratiano and the clown Lancelot Gobbo, and followed in due course by Lorenzo, Jessica, and (in Act V) Antonio; Portia and Nerissa make the same journey in the opposite direction; and Shylock remains in the cold, materialistic world of Venice throughout the play. The conventions of the Elizabethan stage, with continuous action and no fixed scenery, allowed for the rapid alternation of scenes (Venice in Act I, Scene i, Belmont in Act I, Scene ii, Venice in Act I, Scene iii . . .): one reason for the cuts and transpositions in Irving's production and others was the need to allow stagehands time to shift the heavy scenery.

A problem any production or critical interpretation faces is the balance and relative weight of Venice and Belmont, the question of whether the play's disparate elements – fairy-tale and nightmare, comic badinage and the prospect of violent death – can or should cohere. At times, rival critical camps hardly seem to be writing about the same play. One school of critical interpretation, very fashionable in the 1960s and 1970s but less popular recently, sees the play in essentially allegorical terms. Taking Portia's 'quality of mercy' speech as the key to a coherent thematic reading, such critics as Coghill, Lewalski, and Danson view the play as 'written by a Christian for a Christian audience ... about Christian issues': to Danson, Portia's speech in the trial scene 'makes inescapably clear the element of Christian parable with which Shakespeare invested the story'.[17] In this reading of the play, 'the dead letter of the Old Law' is schematically set against the New Testament, the unrepentant flesh against the liberating spirit. Antonio's generosity towards his friend and Portia's 'openness in giving', with no touch of 'crass materialism' in either, exemplify 'the play's central theme of charity or love',[18] and Act V presents an unclouded vision of harmony and reconciliation. For A. D. Moody, on the other hand, 'the play does not celebrate the Christian virtues so much as expose their absence'. In Moody's astringently ironic reading, there is little to choose between Venice and Belmont, both inhabited by materialistic hypocrites, and the principal difference between Shylock and his enemies is that 'Shylock is openly what the Christians are beneath their urbane surface'.[19] To turn the play into a Christian allegory, Moody argues, requires 'a highly selective filter', resolutely ignoring evidence at variance with the preconceived thesis: such an approach 'seems to require us to stand off at some distance from the play', imposing on it an abstract or ideal pattern 'at odds with the experience it actually offers'.[20]

One tendency in recent criticism, as well as in a number of productions of the 1980s and 1990s, has been to deconstruct or complicate the thematic contrast between Belmont and Venice by showing the two as more similar than different. To quote a persuasive recent account by Karen Newman: 'Any simple binary opposition between Belmont and Venice is misleading, for the aristocratic country life of Belmont shares much with commercial Venice ... What is important is the *structure* of exchange itself which characterizes both the economic transactions of Venice and the love relationships forged at Belmont.'[21] Newman, like Walter Cohen, sees the distinction between Belmont and Venice as primarily one of social class, eroded by the dependence of bourgeois and aristocratic societies alike on

6

the cash nexus, as well as on the law of contract which makes financial transactions possible. As Antonio puts it, ruefully, 'the trade and profit of the city' are dependent on confidence in the unvarying 'course of law' (III. iii. 26, 30). Newman's essay, with its emphasis on the use of 'commercial language to describe love relationships',[22] treats Portia rather than Shylock as the play's central figure. A concern with ideology also animates Cohen's subtle Marxist commentary, which attempts 'to view the play as a symptom of a problem in the life of late sixteenth-century England', embodying the cultural contradictions of nascent capitalism. The problematic aspects of the play, to Cohen, result from the 'intractability' of the historical conditions it depicts: 'dramatic form, as a product of an ideological reworking of history, functions to resolve those contradictions that prove irreconcilable in life'.[23]

A number of recent productions of *The Merchant of Venice* present a world where, despite surface distinctions, money rules. Portia's question in the trial scene, 'Which is the merchant here? and which the Jew?' (IV. i. 170), takes on particular resonance in a production like that of Jonathan Miller in 1970, where Olivier's Shylock is 'one among many businessmen, scarcely distinguishable from them' either in dress or in manner.[24]. This production made a conscious attempt to 'demystify, even debunk' Belmont, showing Portia's comfortable surroundings as overtly 'the product of money', a 'mirror into which Venetians look to see their own greed prettily reflected'.[25] A number of productions since that time have followed its example and undercut any binary oppositions by making the two locations equally harsh and unpleasant. Several recent productions, expressionist or quasi-Brechtian, have presented a callow and materialistic Bassanio, seemingly incapable of choosing the leaden casket over the gold.

As the play's theatrical and critical history shows, Portia has proved no less problematical than Shylock to interpreters. Critics and directors have differed widely in what they make of the casket scene and the scenes with Bassanio's rival suitors, while the trial scene, the disguised Portia's moment of triumph, has also prompted a variety of responses. Hazlitt remarks, tartly: 'Portia is not a very great favourite with us . . .

Portia has a certain degree of affectation and pedantry about her ... We do not admire the scene with the caskets'.[26] Partisans of Shylock, like Hazlitt, tend to be unfavourably disposed towards Portia, and vice versa. In production, it is difficult to get the balance right between the two main plot lines and the two leading roles. Irving's famous Victorian production is one of many that have sought by one means or another 'to suppress the romance of the casket plot in favour of the bond plot'.[27] Act V has posed especially difficult problems for directors and critics: how can one keep the return to Belmont, following the high drama of the trial scene, from seeming anticlimactic? Critics have disagreed violently over the tone of Act V – harmony or discord, romantic sentiment or barbed jokes about cuckoldry? – and it has often been claimed that the play is flawed structurally, with only a few loose ends to clear up after the departure of its principal character near the end of Act IV. On the other hand, Newman, Belsey, and other recent critics see Act V as central to the play, and their interpretations find the motifs of casket, bond, and ring to be subtly interconnected.

There can be no single correct interpretation of a literary text, especially of a dramatic text that must, over and over again, be realized in performance. Laurence Olivier's or Henry Goodman's Shylock, or for that matter the Shylock of W. H. Auden, in an essay I admire greatly, can be only one version among many. Readers of this book will no doubt want to construct their own Shylocks, Antonios, and Portias: the artist, as Chekhov says, asks questions rather than trying to give answers.

1

Strangers and Venetians

> The Jew is one whom other men consider a Jew: that is
> the simple truth from which we must start ... It is the
> anti-Semite who *makes* the Jew ... Anti-Semitism is the
> expression of a primitive society that, though secret and
> diffused, remains latent in the legal collectivity.
>
> (Sartre)[1]

I

Sixteenth-century Venice differed from the England of Shakespeare's day in having a substantial Jewish population. There
were money-lenders in Elizabethan England, frequently ex-
coriated as cruel and bloodthirsty usurers, but no Jews were
among them. The handful of Jews in sixteenth-century London
were Marranos, professing Christianity though in some cases
secretly practising their own religion behind closed doors.
Shapiro estimates that there were less than 200 Marranos in
Shakespeare's England (merchants, physicians, musicians,
mostly of Portuguese Sephardic origin), in a population that
included 10,000 aliens.[2] In Venice, on the other hand, Jews
were allowed to practise their religion openly, as a legally
constituted 'estate of outcastes, lower in status than all the
recognized Christian orders', with 'specific privileges and
obligations' and a recognized role in Venetian society.[3] Pro-
hibited from most occupations and from owning land, the Jews
were the bankers of Venice, as well as pawnbrokers and
old-clothes merchants. Jewish money-lenders were tolerated in
Venice for pragmatic reasons, as serving a necessary function
in the economy of a city devoted to trade: 'The employment of
Jewish money-lenders was a profitable, perhaps even a legit-

9

imate, alternative to conniving at Christan usury. At the same time it meant settling in one's city a group of defenseless aliens whose relationship with the Christian majority was permanently uneasy.'[4]

Observers frequently commented on the large number of foreigners or 'strangers' in Venice: with some exaggeration, the French ambassador Commynes said that 'most of their people are foreigners'.[5] The English traveller Thomas Coryat, writing of the magnificent spectacle of St Mark's Square, marvelled at the cosmopolitan splendor of Venice: 'Here you may both see all manner of fashions of attire, and heare all the languages of Christendome, besides those that are spoken by the barbarous Ethnickes; the frequencie of people being so great . . . that (as an elegant writer saith of it) a man may very properly call it rather *Orbis* than *Urbis forum*, that is, a market place of the world, not of the citie.'[6] Gaspare Contarini, in his celebrated *The Commonwealth and Government of Venice* (probably known to Shakespeare in Lewis Lewkenor's English translation),[7] uses similar terms in presenting Venice as a great centre of international trade, remarkable not only for the 'unmeasurable . . . quantity of all sorts of merchandise to be brought out of all realms and countries into this Citie' but for 'the wonderful concourse of strange and forraine people, yea of the farthest and remotest nations, as though the City of *Venice* onely were a common and generall market for the whole world'.[8] Indeed, in a debate in Parliament in 1593 on proposed restrictions on the number of aliens to be permitted in London, one of the speakers explicitly cited Venice as a model for England to follow: 'This Bill should be ill for London, for the riches and renown of the City cometh by entertaining strangers, and giving liberty unto them. Antwerp and Venice could never have been so rich and famous but by entertaining of strangers, and by that means have gained all the intercourse of the world.'[9]

Contarini's idealized account of the Venetian constitution, enormously influential in creating the myth of Venice, places particular emphasis on Venetian justice as 'pure and uncorrupted', scrupulous and unbiased in the execution of the law.

First therefore among the Venetians this alwaies have been most constantly observed, that justice should be equally administred to all, and that it be not lawfull for any how great soever, to doe wrong or injurie to the least of the lower or meanest people, in so much that it hath alwaies been held as a haynous abhomination, & detestable sacriledge, for any gentleman to misuse a Plebeian ... and so much greater was his punishment as hee himself was greater in degree or estimation.[10]

Not only, it was claimed, was 'the city ... open to foreigners, and all could come and go everywhere without any obstacle', but Venetian justice made no distinction between Venetians and outsiders. The diarist Sanuto, citing the case of a judgment in favour of a Florentine against a Venetian patrician, writes: 'The justice of Venetians is excellent, for notwithstanding some controversies with the Florentines, judgment was made against our patrician, a thing not otherwise done'.[11] Venice's reputation for strict and impartial justice is emphasized throughout *The Merchant of Venice*, as is the role of contractual obligation in a society dependent on trade. As Antonio says, after his friend Solanio expresses his hope that 'the duke | Will never grant this forfeiture to hold' (III. iii. 24–5):

> The duke cannot deny the course of law:
> For the commodity that strangers have
> With us in Venice, if it be denied,
> Will much impeach the justice of the state,
> Since that the trade and profit of the city
> Consisteth of all nations.

(III. iii. 26–31)

The economic health of the city, the maintenance of its position as 'a market place of the world', the merchant Antonio tells his friend, is inseparably linked with its reputation as a place where 'strangers' will be afforded fair and just treatment: profit and justice go hand in hand.

The role of the Duke in the trial scene, in which he presides, but acts in a way that clearly is circumscribed, seeing his authority as 'curbed & restrained with lawes', accords with Contarini's account of Venice as a state where 'the course of law' and not the will of man rules.[12] The Duke does not render judgment himself, but defers to the 'learned doctor' Bellario, or his substitute (the disguised Portia), to 'determine' the case under 'the Venetian law' (IV. i. 105–6, 174). Bassanio, with

11

characteristic moral flexibility, suggests to Portia that she 'wrest once the law to your authority, – | To do a great right, do a little wrong', but Portia, more aware of what is appropriate to 'this strict court of Venice', sternly announces 'It must not be, there is no power in Venice | Can alter a decree established' (IV. i, 200, 211–15). Contarini, praising the Venetian constitution, says that the Duke, acting in the interest of 'the common good & civill union', has the power to sit as a full member of any Venetian court hearing a particular case, but may not 'abuse his authoritie' in assuming precedence over his fellow judges or bending them to his will:

> For so great is the princes authoritie, that he may in whatsoever court adjoine himself to the Magistrate therein . . . as his colleague or companion, and have equall power with the other Presidents, that he might so by this meanes be able to looke into all things. Yet nevertheles so is this authoritie of his by lawes retracted, that alone he may not doe any thing, neither being joyned to the other magistrates hath he any farther power then every other president in his office . . . Whereby I thinke any man may easily understand, that the Duke of *Venice* is deprived of all meanes, whereby he might abuse his authoritie, or become a tyrant.[13]

One aspect of the myth of Venice not especially prominent in *The Merchant of Venice* is the praise of the Venetian state as a republic, 'perpetually flourishing & unblemished',[14] which, as Contarini presented it, united the advantages and avoided the disadvantages of monarchical, aristocratic, and democratic forms of government. 'The serene Venetian state' is not in *The Merchant of Venice* set forth as a model for England, 'the fittest pattern on Earth both for direction and imitation', as it was for English republican theorists in the mid and late seventeenth century.[15] But the state of Venice in both *The Merchant of Venice* and *Othello* is explicitly not a monarchy, not a state where tyrants can rule unchecked, and thus differs markedly from the court societies depicted in *The Winter's Tale*, Act I of *As You Like It*, and *Hamlet*, or in such Jacobean plays as *The White Devil* and *The Duchess of Malfi*.

The Venice of Shylock, Antonio, and Bassanio is also a state that recognizes the rights of aliens, coexisting with native Venetians while preserving a distinct identity, but never treated as equals: separate status recognized by law does not imply full equality, and leaves little scope for the assimilation of the outsider into Venetian society. A particularly effective moment at the very end of the 1999 National Theatre *Merchant* (a directorial touch perhaps not entirely warranted by the text) left the converted Jessica, standing apart on centre stage, mourning for the world she had lost and excluded from the community of Venetian Christians.

> In the eyes of churchmen, Jews could be accommodated in a Christian community as long as they were manifestly in it but not of it, and were segregated in such a way as to forestall the pollution of Christianity by Judaism, to discourage any form of undue intimacy between Christian and Jew, and to emphasize the hierarchical relationship between Christianity and Judaism ... Sharing meals, sleeping under the same roof, sexual relationships and any form of association implying equality, hospitality or mutual acceptance: all these things, if not specifically forbidden, were at least highly suspect.[16]

The word 'ghetto' does not appear in *The Merchant of Venice*, and it is unlikely that Shakespeare was aware that Jews in Venice were by legislation restricted to a particular area and not permitted to live elsewhere. But an important exchange between Bassanio and Shylock in Act I, Scene iii clearly indicates that Shakespeare was aware of Jewish dietary laws and their role in fostering the sense of identity and separateness among practising Jews. As a non-Christian alien, Shylock is conscious of his inferior status as depised Other in the eyes of the dominant Christians (demonstrated a moment later, when Antonio says 'I am as like to call thee so again, | To spet on thee again, to spurn thee too' (I. iii. 125–6)). Shylock, referred to again and again in the play as 'the Jew', both excludes and is excluded. Antonio and Shylock reciprocally use the language of pollution, each defining the Other as unclean.

> BASS. If it please you to dine with us.
> SHY. Yes, to smell pork, to eat of the habitation which your prophet the Nazarite conjured the devil into: I will buy with you, sell with you, talk with you, walk with you, and so following: but I will not eat with you, drink with you, nor pray with you.
>
> (I. iii. 28–33)

13

As Shapiro has pointed out, the presence of aliens or 'strangers' in London was a matter of some controversy at the time when Shakespeare was writing *The Merchant of Venice*. In 1593, Queen Elizabeth ordered London authorities to make 'diligent search ... within all parts within your ward what and how many foreigners are residing and remaining within the same, of what nation, profession, trade or occupation every of them are of'. According to one contemporary account, it 'was commonly urged against the strangers, that a greater number might repair hither, than with good policy were fit to be endured'. The alleged 'great multitude of strangers' aroused fears among Londoners, as conspiring 'to rob the English of their commodities to enrich themselves' and, more specifically, as embodying an economic threat to the livelihood of native English 'artisans and mechanical persons' who 'might be impoverished' by competition with these foreigners.[17] In 1595, a mob of over 1,000 apprentices and 'poor tradesmen' rioted at Tower Hill, demanding the expulsion of 'the strangers' and attacking them physically, and it was the marks of separateness among the aliens that particularly aroused their animosity: 'though they be demized or born here among us, yet they keep themselves severed from us in church, in government, in trade, in language and in marriage'.[18] The animosity towards Shylock expressed in *The Merchant of Venice* by Salerio, Solanio, Gratiano, and Antonio is fuelled by a similar assertion of tribal solidarity against the demonized Other, implicitly denying Shylock's claim that a Jew is 'warmed and cooled by the same winter and summer as a Christian is' (III. i. 56–8).

> SHY. I say my daughter is my flesh and my blood.
> SAL. There is more difference between thy flesh and hers, than between jet and ivory, than there is between red wine and Rhenish.
>
> (III. i. 34–6)

A scene from the play *Sir Thomas More*, the only surviving literary manuscript in Shakespeare's own hand, depicts an earlier anti-alien riot, with the aim of 'the removing of the strangers, which cannot choose but advantage the poor handicrafts of the city'. More, then Sheriff of London, addresses the unruly mob in terms that recall both Ulysses' speech on order and degree in *Troilus and Cressida* and the treatment of strangers and Venetians in *The Merchant of Venice*:

> Imagine that you see the wretched strangers,
> Their babies at their backs, with their poor luggage
> Plodding to th' ports and coasts for transportation,
> And that you sit as kings in your desires,
> Authority quite silenc'd by your brawl,
> And you in ruff of your opinions cloth'd,
> What had you got? I'll tell you: you had taught
> How insolence and strong hand should prevail,
> How order should be quell'd . . .
>   .   .   .   .   .   .
>   Men like ravenous fishes
> Would feed on one another.

(Addition II, ll. 74–82, 86–7)

More's appeal to common humanity, to the sympathies that unite rather than divide those of differing traditions and allegiances, anticipates the argument of Shylock's 'Hath not a Jew eyes? hath not a Jew hands, organs, dimensions, senses, affections, passions?' (III. i. 52–4). Both passages direct their rhetorical force against the violent tribal antagonisms expressed by many of the characters in *The Merchant of Venice* – in Shylock's 'But yet I'll go in hate, to feed upon | The prodigal Christian' no less than in Solanio's 'Here comes another of the tribe – a third cannot be match'd, unless the devil himself turn Jew' (II. v. 14–15; III. i. 70–1).

More's powerful invocation of the universal wolf of anarchic disorder, to remind the rebellious mob of the possible consequences of their action, is followed, later in the scene, by an appeal to self-interest. What if the same thing were to happen to you? What if you, by a sudden change of fortune, were to become a stranger?

> You'll put down strangers,
> Kill them, cut their throats, possess their houses,
> And lead the majesty of law in lyam   [on a leash]
> To slip him like a hound; alas, alas, say now the King . . .
>   .   .   .   .   .   .
> Should so much come so short of your great trespass
> As but to banish you, whither would you go?
> What country by the nature of your error

15

> Should give you harbor? Go you to France or Flanders,
> To any German province, Spain or Portigal,
> Nay, any where that not adheres to England,
> Why, you must needs be strangers; would you be pleas'd
>   To find a nation of such barbarous temper
> That breaking out in hideous violence
>   Would not afford you an abode on earth[?]
> .   .   .   .   .   .
>   What would you think
> To be thus us'd?
>
>   (Addition II, ll. 119–33, 139–40)

The catalogue of humiliating abuses that More suggests strangers are likely to endure includes details directly echoed in the exchange between Shylock and Antonio in *The Merchant of Venice*, Act I, Scene iii:

> MORE. Spurn you like dogs, and like as if that God
>   Owed not nor made not you, nor that the elements
>   Were not all appropriate for your comforts,
>   But charter'd unto them.
>
>   (Addition II, ll. 136–9)

> SHY. You call me misbeliever, cut-throat dog,
>   And spet upon my Jewish gaberdine,
>   And all for use of that which is mine own . . .
>   .   .   .   .   .   .
>   Shall I bend low, and in a bondman's key
>   With bated breath, and whisp'ring humbleness
>   Say this:
>   'Fair sir, you spet on me on Wednesday last,
>   You spurn'd me such a day, another time
>   You call'd me dog: and for these courtesies
>   I'll lend you thus much moneys'?
>
>   (I. iii. 106–8, 118–24)

As Sartre says in his illuminating account of the psychology of anti-Semitism quoted as an epigraph to this chapter, 'the Jew is one whom other men consider a Jew . . . It is the anti-Semite who *makes* the Jew'. Cultural identity is forged by rejection and exclusion, but, as More's address to the angry Londoners suggests, imaginative empathy can, for the moment at least, transcend tribal loyalties.

16

II

Attitudes toward usury, or the lending of money at interest, were more complex and varied in Elizabethan England than is often supposed. Though preachers fulminated against usury as contrary to God's law, Parliament in 1571 passed a law fixing the rate of interest at 10 per cent, more or less on the Venetian model. Antonio in *The Merchant of Venice* argues the traditional position, as set forth in such anti-usury tracts as Miles Mosse's *The Arraignment and Conviction of Usury* (1595) and Thomas Wilson's *A Discourse upon Usury* (1572): 'I neither lend nor borrow | By taking nor by giving of excess.' He is willing to advance money to oblige a friend (Shylock calls it 'low simplicity' that Antonio 'lends out money gratis', thus driving down 'the rate of usance' among Shylock's fellow professional money-lenders), but he expects only the repayment of principal, and is even willing to cancel the debt if the debtor, like Bassanio, finds it difficult 'to get clear of all the debts' he owes (I. i. 134; I. iii. 38–40, 56–7). Wilson, like other traditional moralists who found the charging of interest on loans distasteful, equated usury with theft: 'He that taketh over and above that he lendeth is an usurer, and so a synner before god, as he that stealeth but a penny by the hygh way is a theefe as well as he that stealeth an hundreth pound, and worthy to be hanged therefore.'[19] Yet Wilson's *Discourse* takes the form of a dialogue, in which this rigorous condemnation of the charging of any interest, however small, is contrasted with another position, argued by a lawyer and a merchant, justifying the lending of money at an authorized rate of interest, which would allow the lender a reasonable return on his investment:

> If some one man pay moderatedly over and above, for that which he hath borrowed, I say it is no offence before god, as I take it. And recompense is allowed for beneefites donne, saye what you will . . .
>
> For, I pray you, what trade or bargayning can there be among marchants, or what lending or borrowinge among al men, if you take awaye the assurance and the hope of gayne? What man is so madde to deliver his moneye out of his owne possession for naughte? . . . or who is hee that will lende to others and want him self?[20]

The prudential case for 'the commodities of usury' is stated dispassionately in Francis Bacon's essay 'Of Usury' (1625), in which he uses the term in an ethically neutral way, without the moral opprobrium often attached to it. 'It is a vanity to conceive that there would be ordinary borrowing without profit, and it is impossible to conceive the number of inconveniences that will ensue if borrowing be cramped. Therefore to speak of the abolishing of usury is idle: all states have ever had it, in one kind or rate or other.'[21] The distinction normally made by those who, like Bacon and many of the speakers in the parliamentary debate on the 1571 statute, advocated the regulation of the rate of interest rather than, like the Preacher in Wilson's *Discourse*, urging that that there be 'as straite lawes to forbid usurie, as there bee to forbid felony or murder',[22] is that between 'biting' or exorbitant usury and interest charged at a moderate rate. As Nelson has pointed out in *The Idea of Usury*, this distinction finds support in a number of statements by Calvin and other Reformed Protestant theologians.[23] When Shylock objects that Antonio 'calls interest' what Shylock himself characterizes with such honorific terms as 'my bargains, and my well-won thrift', he is justifying his own activities as 'a way to thrive' no different from any other: 'And thrift is blessing if men steal it not' (I. iii. 45–6, 84–5). The trade of Venice – and of London – was dependent on the availability of credit, what Tawney in his introduction to Wilson's *Discourse* describes as 'the need of large sums to finance the purchase of the produce handled on the world markets'.[24] As Bacon says:

> It is certain that the greatest part of trade is driven by young merchants upon borrowing at interest; so as if the usurer either call in or keep back his money, there will ensue presently a great stand of trade ... Were it not for this easy borrowing upon interest, men's necessities would draw upon them a most sudden undoing, in that they would be forced to sell their means (be it land or goods) far under foot; and so, where as usury does but gnaw upon them, bad markets would swallow them quite up.[25]

The passage in Deuteronomy that stigmatizes usury as contrary to God's law carefully distinguishes between lending to a brother and lending to a stranger: 'Thou shalt not lend upon usury to thy brother; usury of money, usury of victuals, usury of any thing that is lent upon usury: Unto a stranger thou mayest lend upon usury; but unto thy brother thou shalt not lend upon usury.' (Deut. 23: 19–20). This distinction forbids Jews from charging interest on loans to their fellow Jews (thus Tubal advances the sum of 3,000 ducats to Shylock, whose 'present store' is not sufficient for him to cover the loan to Antonio), but permits Shylock, an observant Jew, to charge interest to the non-Jew Antonio. Conversely, since the biblical passage was generally held to apply to borrowing as well as lending money, Antonio, if he were to follow a strict interpretation of the passage, would be happy to advance money freely to his friend and fellow Christian Bassanio, but, with some reluctance, is willing to 'try what my credit can in Venice do' and 'break a custom' in order to 'supply the ripe wants of my friend' by standing surety to his friend's loan, agreeing to pay interest to the non-Christian and non-Venetian 'stranger' Shylock (I. i. 180; I. iii. 58–9).

One traditional patristic interpretation of the distinction between strangers and brothers, that of St Ambrose, seems surprisingly vengeful in tone, defining all strangers, all outside the tribe, as enemies: 'Who, then, is the stranger? the foe of God's people. From him, demand usury whom you rightly desire to harm, against whom weapons are lawfully carried. Upon him usury is legally imposed. Where there is a right of war, there is also the right of usury.'[26] Antonio, expressing deep-seated animosity towards Shylock, makes a similar distinction between lending to a friend, as an active manifestation of mutual sympathy, and lending to an enemy, from whom one could exact any penalty incurred without compunction. Unwittingly, he has given Shylock the opportunity to do just that in the later action of the play, when Shylock treats him not simply as a debtor in a contractual relationship, but as an enemy, against whom he is in a perpetual state of war. The rigid polarization implicit in Antonio's speech – anyone not my friend is my enemy – is fully reciprocated by Shylock, both in his conduct during this scene and in his pursuit of revenge later.

> ANT. If thou wilt lend this money, lend it not
> As to thy friends, for when did friendship take
> A breed for barren metal of his friend?

19

> But lend it rather to thine enemy,
> Who if he break, thou may'st with better face
> Exact the penalty.

(I. iii. 127–32)

The irony in Shylock's response, 'I would be friends with you, and have your love', as he offers the 'merry bond' of the pound of flesh, is entirely lost on Antonio and Bassanio, who take his words at face value. Antonio thinks he shows 'much kindness', behaving as friend not enemy ('the Hebrew will turn Christian'), and even Bassanio, more suspicious, considers these to be 'fair terms' (I. iii. 134, 149, 169, 174–5).

The merchant Antonio's unstinting generosity towards his friend Bassanio, his unhesitating readiness 'to submit the rights of commerce to the claims of love', even to the extent of risking his own life,[27] can be seen as embodying another interpretation of the biblical prohibition of usury. If all men are brothers, if the ideal of universal love, as set forth in the Sermon on the Mount, transcends tribal loyalties, then the passage in Deuteronomy can be read as promoting a wide-ranging benevolence. Auden cites a passage from St Thomas Aquinas as representative: 'The Jews were forbidden to take usury from their brethren, i.e., from other Jews. By this we are given to understand that to take usury from any man is simply evil, because we ought to treat every man as our neighbor and brother, especially in the state of the Gospel whereto we are called.'[28] Those critics like Brown and Danson who see the play in schematic terms, often finding in it an element of Christian parable, tend to contrast, on one side of the equation, Portia and Antonio, selfless and generous in giving their 'uttermost' both in 'purse' and in 'person' – 'You shall have gold | To pay the petty debt twenty times over' (I. i. 138, 156; III. ii. 305–6) – with a Shylock devoted to 'wholly commercial transactions in which gain is the object, enforcement the method, and even human beings are merely things to be possessed'.[29]

Yet the view of Shylock as embodiment of the cash nexus, or of the play as a whole as representing a 'contemptuous abhorrence' of usury and usurers supposedly characteristic of the Elizabethan period,[30] robs the play of much of its complexity. Shylock himself points out in proposing the bond to

Antonio that he is not motivated wholly by the calculation of material gain and loss.

> If he should break his day what should I gain
> By the exaction of the forfeiture?
> A pound of man's flesh taken from a man,
> Is not so estimable, profitable neither
> As flesh of muttons, beefs, or goats.

(I. iii. 159–63)

When Bassanio characterizes his friendship to Antonio as indebtedness 'in money and in love' (I. i. 131) or when he mentions Portia's wealth before her beauty and 'wondrous virtues', comparing the quest to gain her with the pursuit of the golden fleece (I. i. 131, 161–3, 170–2), he shows a marked inability to disentangle love or friendship from the pursuit of economic advantage. Even in the casket scene, where Bassanio makes the right choice in recognizing the potential deceptiveness of 'outward shows', rejecting 'gaudy gold' and silver for 'meagre lead' (III. ii. 73, 101–4), he is fully aware, as is Portia, that the prize at stake is Portia's wealth as much as her person. By the stipulations of her father's will, Portia and the wealth she has inherited are 'lock'd' within a casket, the symbolic equivalent of the 'casket ... worth the pains', containing Shylock's gold and jewels, which the disobedient Jessica, gilded with ducats, bestows on Lorenzo (II. vi. 33, 49–50; III. ii. 40). In *The Merchant of Venice*, 'hardly any relationship between two characters is left as solely emotional or erotic', without an explicit economic component; it is 'a play in which Eros and Mammon are closely intertwined'.[31] Portia and Antonio, no less than Shylock, consistently use the language of economic exchange to express the emotions of reciprocal or thwarted love. 'Since you are dear bought, I will love you dear', Portia tells Bassanio, immediately after reminding him how extensive her financial resources are, enough to 'double six thousand, and then treble that' (III. ii. 299, 312).

In the trial scene, Antonio and Bassanio compete in the offers they make one another to testify their mutual love, and both by implication elevate the idealized friendship of this homosocial bond as exceeding the love of man for woman, even as sanctified by marriage.

21

ANT. Commend me to your honourable wife,
  Tell her the process of Antonio's end,
  Say how I lov'd you, speak me fair in death:
  And when the tale is told, bid her be judge
  Whether Bassanio had not once a love.
  .   .   .   .   .   .

BASS. Antonio, I am married to a wife
  Which is as dear to me as life itself,
  But life itself, my wife, and all the world,
  Are not with me esteem'd above thy life.
  I would lose all, ay sacrifice them all
  Here to this devil, to deliver you.

(IV. i. 269–84)

The pathos and nobility of sentiment in Antonio's lines, spoken when he is fully reconciled to and even welcomes death, are undercut somewhat by the crass boastfulness of Bassanio's rejoinder, offering not to sacrifice his own life but someone else's (even hinting at an offer of his wife's sexual services to Shylock as a bribe). The comic astringency of Portia's ironic comment, rendered cryptic by her disguise, deflates the pretensions of a male solidarity that treats men as brothers at the expense of devaluing women.

Your wife would give you little thanks for that
If she were by to hear you make the offer.

(IV. i. 284–5)

Much of the action of Act V, with its bawdy puns and sexual byplay, is foreshadowed by the interjections of the two disguised women, Portia and Nerissa, who suggest to their fallible husbands that 'an unquiet house' (IV. i. 290) might well be the consequence of competing affections and loyalties, and of the assumption that human beings, male or female, could be treated simply as transferable property.

In Portia's 'quality of mercy' speech, mercy, freely given without calculation of advantage, is contrasted with 'compulsion' or constraint. In some respects, this speech is a straightforward exposition of an ideal of universal brotherhood, with all human beings, debtor and creditor ('him that gives, and him that takes'(VI. i. 183)), Christian and Jew, the mightiest monarch and the humblest subject, equal before God. The repeated pronouns 'we' and 'us', in lines addressed to Shylock, are inclusive rather than positing an assumed community from which Shylock and other strangers are excluded. Yet the lines address Shylock as 'Jew', advancing arguments that are explicitly Christian in their doctrinal and liturgical assumptions.

> Therefore Jew,
> Though justice be thy plea, consider this,
> That in the course of justice, none of us
> Should see salvation: we do pray for mercy,
> And that same prayer, doth teach us all to render
> The deeds of mercy.
>
> (IV. i. 193–8)

The allusion here is to the Lord's Prayer (an intrinsic part of Christian church services, which Shylock would neither wish nor be permitted to attend), and the contrast of strict Old Testament morality and a new dispensation by which, by Christ's intercession, sins will be forgiven, is central not only to these lines but to the trial scene in general.[32] Shylock's defiant response 'My deeds upon my head! I crave the law' (IV. i. 202) affirms the Old Law, insisting on strict and unrelenting judgment and redefining 'deeds' in terms of retribution rather than mercy. The chilling echo of Matthew 27: 25, 'His blood be on us, and on our children', suggests a willed exclusion from any Christian consensus on Shylock's part, whatever the consequences, as he chooses instead to affirm solidarity with what he later calls 'the stock of Barrabas' (IV. i. 292).

By the end of the trial scene, retribution has been exacted, but on Shylock the alien rather than on the Venetian merchant. In a twist to the plot with no parallel in any of the play's sources and analogues, Portia suddenly invokes a law not mentioned in the earlier stages of the trial.

> The law hath yet another hold on you.
> It is enacted in the laws of Venice,
> If it be proved against an alien,
> That by direct, or indirect attempts
> He seek the life of any citizen,
> The party 'gainst the which he doth contrive,
> Shall seize one half his goods, the other half

> Comes to the privy coffer of the state,
> And the offender's life lies in the mercy
> Of the Duke only.

(IV. i. 343–52)

Shylock's status as alien, as potential threat to the health of the body politic, is made painfully apparent by a law that demonstrates to him how precarious his position in Venetian society can be. As Auden says, 'we are reminded that, irrespective of his personal character, his status is one of inferiority. A Jew is not regarded, even in law, as a brother'.[33] The forced conversion shortly afterwards, by which, in return for sparing his life and remitting part of the fine, he is told he 'must presently become a Christian' (IV. i. 383), is by no means a manifestation of mercy or of impartial justice. Rather than admitting him into a community of believers, this change of religion by compulsion is a final, crushing humiliation, stripping Shylock not only of 'the prop | That doth sustain my house . . . | the means whereby I live' (IV. i. 371–3), but of his identity as a Jew, a member of a tolerated minority of strangers.

2

Some Versions of Shylock

I

We know very little about how Shylock was portrayed in the
original Elizabethan production, which, according to the 1600
Quarto, was 'divers times acted by the Lord Chamberlaine his
Servants'. Though Stoll's confident assertion that Shylock was
initially played as a comic character, with a red wig, red beard,
and exaggerated hooked nose, has been echoed by several later
critics, there is virtually no contemporary evidence to support
Stoll's assumption.[1] It has been suggested that Thomas Pope, a
shareholder and principal actor in the Chamberlain's Men,
about 40 years old in 1596, playing both serious and comic
roles (one contemporary account speaks of him as '*Pope* the
Clowne'), was the first Shylock, and that after Pope's death in
1603 the role was taken over by John Lowin. Lowin is known
to have played Bosola, Sir Epicure Mammon, and Henry VIII,
and probably was the original Iago, where Pope may have
played Falstaff, Jaques, and Falconbridge, as well as Shylock.[2]
But all this is conjecture, based on limited evidence. What we
do know is that the play remained in the repertory of
Shakespeare's company (though it was not as popular as *The
Jew of Malta*, acted by several different companies between 1502
and 1600), and that in 1604, after the accession of James I, it
was the only play to receive two performances, at the request
of the King, in a brief season of plays acted at court.

In 1701, George Granville, Lord Lansdowne, adapted Shakespeare's play as *The Jew of Venice*, and here Shylock is definitely
a comic character. In the revision, which professes to correct
'the first rude Sketches' of Shakespeare, adding a 'nobler

25

Lustre', the part of Bassanio is fattened, to accommodate Thomas Betterton, the leading actor of the company at Lincoln's Inn Fields, giving him a number of high-flown speeches in praise of sacred friendship.[3] In the cast list, Bassanio is listed first, Antonio second, and Shylock fifth. The part of Shylock was taken by Thomas Doggett, the company's low comedian, described by contemporaries as 'wearing a Farce in his face' and particularly skilful in make-up and costume, 'dressing a character to the greatest Exactness'.[4] Granville's Shylock lacks dignity and complexity, 'not a Shylock who was likely to inspire much fear'.[5] A characteristic interpolation by Granville is a banquet scene in which, after toasts by Antonio, Bassanio, and Gratiano, Shylock says:

> I have a Mistress, that out-shines 'em all . . .
> O may her Charms encrease and multiply;
> My Money is my Mistress! Here's to
> Interest upon Interest.   [*Drinks.*
>
> (*The Jew of Venice*, II. ii, p. 12)

Actors who followed Doggett in the role, until Charles Macklin in 1741, saw Shylock as a comic villain.[6] When Rowe in 1709 spoke of having seen the play as 'Receiv'd and Acted as a Comedy' with 'the Part of the *Jew* perform'd by an Excellent Comedian', it is Granville's play, not Shakespeare's: no performances of *The Merchant of Venice*, other than in Granville's revised and shortened version, are listed in the *London Stage* for the Restoration period or the early eighteenth century.

When Macklin essayed the role, he restored the Shakespearian text (with some cuts), and reinterpreted the character to make him much more formidable and threatening. In Macklin's performance, according to contemporary accounts, there was 'a forcible and terrifying ferocity . . . such an iron-visaged look, such a relentless, savage cast of manners, that the audience seemed to shrink from the character'.[7] When George II saw Macklin in the role, he was unable to sleep that night. Like Irving a century later, Macklin is said to have prepared himself for the role by observing contemporary Jews in order to 'habituate himself to their air and deportment',[8] and, like a number of twentieth-century Shylocks, he saw Act III, Scene i, and especially the scene with Tubal, as central to an understanding of the character. In this scene, according to the *Memoirs of Charles Macklin*, 'I threw out all my fire ... the contrasted passions of joy for the Merchant's losses, and grief for the elopement of Jessica, open a fine field for an actor's powers'.[9] Macklin's Shylock, a role he continued to play with great acclaim for nearly forty years, was by no means sympathetic, but had the 'savage Fierceness' and unrelenting 'Cruelty' that Rowe, some years earlier, had found more akin to tragedy than comedy.

Edmund Kean's celebrated interpretation of the role, first seen at Drury Lane in 1814, was no less powerful – Coleridge described it as 'like reading Shakespeare by flashes of lightning' – but it was aimed at eliciting sympathy rather than fear in the audience. Kean's performance was characterized by great intensity and rapid emotional transitions: his Shylock was not only dignified, but full of feeling and proud of his Jewish heritage. According to one spectator on the first night, 'his voice swells and deepens at the mention of his sacred tribe and ancient law'. Kean inaugurated the tradition of making 'Hath not a Jew eyes' the heart of the play, pulling out all the stops in his 'passionate recrimination and wild justice of argument'.[10] 'He hurried you on through the catalogue of Antonio's atrocities and unprovoked injuries to him ... and when he had reached the climax, he came down by a sudden transition to a gentle, suffering tone of simple representation of his oppressor's manifest un-reason and injustice on the words, "I am a *Jew*".'[11] This was, as Hazlitt noted, a Shylock more sinned against than sinning, 'brooding over daily insults and injuries' to become 'the depository of the vengeance of his race'.[12]

Henry Irving's Victorian production featured elaborate sets depicting Venetian scenes, sumptuous costumes, massive textual cuts, and a fully tragic Shylock as the play's dominant figure. One reason for this production's enduring popularity was the magnificence of its pictorial setting, modelled after Veronese and other painters of the Venetian school: 'Venice lived again before us, thanks to Irving's scene-painters and costumers, as we had dreamed of it ... the bridges, the palaces, the gondolas, all were there.'[13] Irving saw Shylock as a figure of 'patriarchal dignity', as 'almost the only gentleman in the play and the most ill-used'; in an interview in 1885, he described Shylock as 'a religious Jew' who was 'proud of his descent – conscious of his moral superiority to many of the Christians who scoffed at him'.[14] As actor-manager, Irving reshaped the play to make the ill-used Shylock, described in a review of the original 1879 production as a figure 'who can raise emotion both of pity and fear, and make us Christians thrill with a retrospective sense of shame',[15] the play's dramatic and moral centre. He cut the Belmont scenes considerably, altering the balance of the play: in Bernard Shaw's trenchant phrase, Irving 'does not merely cut plays, he disembowels them'.[16] One scene frequently praised by contemporaries was an interpolation by Irving. Jessica's flight with Lorenzo (Act II, Scene vi) in Irving's production was accompanied with a great deal of stage business – gondolas passing by, dancing pierrots in the moonlight, 'masked revellers, merrily singing' – and then, after the noise had died down, the weary Shylock, carrying a lantern, walked slowly across the empty stage to find his house deserted. The curtain fell on his 'look of dumb and complete despair' at the loss of his daughter. According to Ellen Terry, who played Portia in this production, 'for absolute pathos, achieved by absolute simplicity of means, I never saw anything in the theatre to compare with ... Shylock's return over the bridge to his deserted house after Jessica's flight'.[17]

Other comments by Ellen Terry suggest a certain frustration at a production in which Portia's role was subordinated to that of Shylock, even in the trial scene: 'his heroic saint was splendid, but it wasn't good for Portia'.[18] In the trial scene, Irving's Shylock had a quiet dignity and seemed more victim than aggressor, with an onstage chorus of his fellow Jews subjected to jeering and threats of violence by the assembled Christians. One observer ironically commented that Portia's 'quibbling tricky speeches' seemed 'small and mean ... when addressed to a being who united the soul of Savonarola and the bearing of Charles I'[19] Like Olivier and other recent Shylocks, Irving made much of his final exit, crushed by defeat, uttering 'a long, heavy sigh' as he 'walks away to die in silence and alone'.[20] One dissenter from the general acclaim for Irving's tragic Shylock was Shaw, who saw in him a tendency 'to use other men's plays as the framework for his own creations': 'There was no question then of a bad Shylock or a good Shylock: he was simply not Shylock at all; and when his own creation came into conflict with Shakespear's, as it did quite openly in the Trial scene, he simply played in flat contradiction to the lines, and positively acted Shakespear off the stage.'[21]

II

The National Theatre production of 1970, directed by Jonathan Miller and starring Laurence Olivier as Shylock, did not cut the play as severely as Irving had done, but followed Irving in subordinating the casket plot to the bond plot and making Shylock the play's protagonist. Miller's production set the play in Victorian England, with a Shylock who was an assimilated Jew, rather than an exotic figure immediately set apart in appearance from the other characters. According to Miller, Olivier 'realized the possible advantage of making himself look much more like everyone else, as it is this crucial question of difference that lies at the heart of the play'. The use of the Victorian setting, Miller argued, allowed for 'the possibility of unforeseen meanings' hitherto obscured: 'Transposed into this late nineteenth-century world, the play unavoidably delivered meanings that had been inaudible to me before'.[22]

A young director with a very famous, charismatic actor in the lead role, Miller in 1970 faced a number of interpretative problems: how to treat the relationship between Shylock the alien and Venetian society, and how to present the play's two contrasting physical locations and separate worlds, Venice and Belmont. The 1970 *Merchant* was governed by an overall thematic conception – 'I kept on reminding the cast to highlight this tension between kin and kind, and that the play was a constant subliminal argument about the notions of difference and similarity'[23] – but it was in no sense an ensemble performance, a seamless web. Olivier could adapt himself to the overall tone of the production but he could not stop being a star, giving a performance of extraordinary tragic power (preserved in a 1973 video), and dominating the production, as Kean, Macklin, and Irving had done before him.

Olivier's Jew, a prosperous banker rather than a usurer, initially seeks to ingratiate himself with the Christians, but is always aware that he does not fit in. Venetian society here as in some later productions is presented as smug and hypocritical, a closed world cocooned by money and privilege. In this production, Shylock, overwhelmed with grief and rage at the desertion of his daughter, is the only character who seems capable of expressing emotion. 'I would not have given it for a wilderness of monkeys' (III. i. 112–13), accompanied by stage business involving his dead wife's picture, a sacred family relic, is the emotional high point of Olivier's performance. An unheroic and unromantic Bassanio, in contrast, is coldly manipulative in exploiting a besotted Antonio. Miller, who describes Antonio as 'a sad old queen' in thrall to a younger, heterosexual opportunist,[24] is one of several directors and critics who bring out a homoerotic subtext in the play.

If the prevailing tone of the Venice scenes involving Shylock is tragic in this production, the Belmont scenes are played for laughs, demystifying any element of moonlit romance and fairy tale. The Morocco and Arragon scenes are very funny (particularly the latter, with a senile and half-blind Arragon), but devoid of suspense, allowing no possibility that either of them could choose rightly and conveying little sense that the two suitors are failing a test. Consciously eschewing the Ellen Terry tradition of Portia as warm and impulsive, a romantic heroine, Joan Plowright's Portia is a cool customer, ironic, mature, and uninvolved, comfortably ensconced in the 'tastelessly ornate furnishings' of the prosperous Victorian bourgeoisie.[25] The casket scene becomes an empty, fraudulent charade, in which Portia (playing 'I could teach you | How to choose right, but then I am forsworn' with a nod and a wink) openly prompts Bassanio's answer. The song 'Tell me where is Fancy bred' is turned into farce, with two grotesque operatic sopranos emphasizing the rhymes on 'lead' so heavily that Bassanio would have to be dim-witted to miss the hints. In this production, the trial scene, up to Shylock's defeat, is unusually muted and restrained: one reviewer complained that 'in the long history of *The Merchant of Venice* the trial scene can never have generated so little excitement'.[26] Leaning over backward to avoid 'the sentimental radiance' generally associated with the 'quality of mercy' speech, Portia spoke the lines 'as if having laboriously to explain what should have been self-evident to someone too stupid to understand'.[27]

The problematical role of Jessica in this production was treated in an interesting way, as an outsider unable to find a secure place among either Christians or Jews. In the 1970 *Merchant*, there are few signs of affection between Lorenzo and Jessica, either in Venice or in Belmont (in keeping with the production's anti-romantic tone and emphasis on the cash nexus), and Jessica falls asleep during the middle of Lorenzo's 'How sweet the moonlight sleeps' speech in Act V, Scene i. Though Olivier's Shylock is devastated by his daughter's desertion – 'he had been raped by a pack of Christian dogs', Olivier commented[28] – she shows no comparable attachment to her father. Act V, as in the reading of such critics as Moody and Belsey, is played to emphasize discord rather than harmony. Jessica is made to feel distinctly unwelcome in Belmont, where on two separate occasions Portia forgets (or pretends to forget) her name. And in a striking directorial touch similar in many ways to the final tableau in the 1999 National Theatre production, the play ends with a melancholy Jessica all alone on stage, as the plaintive sounds of the Kaddish, the Hebrew lament for the dead, are heard.

Jonathan Miller was involved in a second production of *Merchant* for BBC television in 1980, in which he served as producer and Jack Gold as director. Here the setting was vaguely Elizabethan, rather than Victorian, and Warren Mitchell played Shylock with a heavy East European 'Yiddish' accent, and without Olivier's tragic dignity. The Belmont scenes, brightly lit, were played in a conventional romantic manner in an outdoor setting. In Venice and in Belmont, there was little of the earlier production's emphasis on the pursuit of financial gain, but instead Miller and Gold sought for a balance of sympathies, treating the play as 'totally symmetrical in its prejudices'.[29] Mitchell, a small man with mobile features and long experience as a television and stage actor, was a seedy, shabby Shylock, and his performance received mixed reviews. 'Hath not a Jew eyes' was played with the diminutive Shylock surrounded by two burly Venetians, jostling and manhandling him: this may have brought out the point of pervasive and brutal Venetian anti-Semitism, but the excessive, heavy-handed stage business made it very hard for the viewers to pay attention to the words being spoken. As in Miller's earlier production, Jessica's role was built up. Here Jessica and Lorenzo were clearly attracted to one another sexually – Gold commented that in Act V 'they have probably been making love to each other non-stop . . . and can't wait to get each other back into bed'[30] – and Jessica, passionately angry in 'Our house is hell' (II. iii. 2) and elsewhere in Act II, unambiguously loathed her father.

The two late-twentieth-century productions of *Merchant* about which the most documentary evidence is available were both directed by John Barton for the Royal Shakespeare Company, in 1978–9 and 1981. The two Shylocks, Patrick Stewart and David Suchet, each gave detailed accounts of the way they approached the role, as did Sinead Cusack, who played Portia in 1981, and there is also a fascinating three-way discussion involving Barton, Stewart, and Suchet in Barton's *Playing Shakespeare* (1984), based on a television programme shown on Channel Four, in which the two Shylocks perform extracts from the play. Both actors playing Shylock were conscious of the heavy weight of encrusted tradition, finding the prospect of 'undertaking 'such a famous part', with its long history of past performance, 'terrifying': 'In acting Shakespeare, past tradition is constantly present. We are bombarded by received impressions: performances we have seen, reviews that we have read. It's very difficult to rid yourself of these impressions and go for something which is original.'[31] Both Stewart and Suchet, hoping to avoid 'the fear of finding oneself trundling along tramlines, trapped in a lifeless mould', sought to approach the part without preconceptions, seeking to interpret the character in new and unfamiliar ways, emphasizing 'the ambiguities and contradictions' in the character of Shylock.[32] What is particularly interesting here is that in what was in many ways a similar production, with the same director and designer (in rehearsal, Barton said, 'basically I gave Patrick and David the same directions and made the same points, both in detail and in general'), the two actors had entirely different conceptions of the role of Shylock, and on stage 'the result was utterly different and individual'.[33]

One major difference, noted again and again in reviews, was in their physical appearance and dress. Stewart's Shylock wore a frayed, stained coat and battered shoes, rolling his own cigarettes and saving the butt-ends for future use, showing an 'excessive meanness' which verged on obsession: 'I wore a shabby, dirty broken-down frock-coat, because I think that the most important thing for Shylock in the play is money, possessions and finance. I thought that if he was obsessed with money he would not waste it on how he appeared. So I made an attempt to make my Shylock very shabby and down at heel.'[34] Like such recent critics as Walter Cohen and Karen Newman, Stewart gave emphasis to the desire for material security as an 'aid to survival' and as something that 'seems to dominate and colour relationships' in the play. In his interpretation, Shylock's 'obsession with the retention and acquisition of wealth' brought about a deforming 'imbalance', drying up any capacity he might have had for human sympathy, warmth, or affection, apparent in his cold and loveless household no less than in his dealings with a hostile Venetian society: 'there is a bleak and terrible loneliness in Shylock which I suspect is the cause of much of his anger and bitterness.'[35]

Though Suchet (and presumably Barton as director) agreed that a dominating concern with monetary transactions – 'his thoughts are all on the Stock Exchange and banking and money' – helped to explain Shylock's motivation throughout the play, and that in the scene with Jessica (Act II, Scene v), so important in defining his character and values, 'there's hardly any word of endearment to his daughter',[36] his Shylock was in other respects very different. The 1981 Shylock was well-dressed, prosperous, dignified, a banker or a businessman rather than a miserly usurer, yet capable of anger and resentment that he was only rarely able to express. One major difference was that Suchet, a Jew himself, emphasized Shylock's Jewish identity – 'my Shylock was very proud of his Jewishness. Why should he hide it?' – where Stewart, far more than any previous Shylock, sought to play down this aspect of the play, seeing 'the Jewishness which is so often emphasized in *The Merchant* as . . . a distraction'. 'Whenever I've seen a very ethnic, a very Jewish Shylock, I've felt that something's been missing. Shylock is essentially an alien, an outsider. I think if you see him as a Jew, first and foremost, then he's in danger of becoming only a symbol. Shylock is an outsider who happens to be a Jew.'[37] Suchet, in contrast, considered 'the Jewish element in the play' as 'unavoidable and very important', with Shylock, in his family and business relationships, defining himself as a Jew in a society where Jews are by law considered inferiors: 'Shakespeare never lets the audience or the other characters forget the Jewish thing. You only have to look at the trial scene where he's called "Shylock" only six times but 'Jew' twenty-two.'[38]

In each of the five scenes in which Shylock appeared, Stewart and Suchet, with their differing conceptions of the part, sought to 'look into each scene for exactly what it was, for what it said to me, and to play that'.[39] As the history of performance and criticism of this play shows, 'what it was' varies greatly, according to the perceptions of the individual actor or critic – Rowe and Hazlitt; Macklin and Kean; Danson, Moody, and Shapiro. Suchet, described in one review as the funniest Shylock as well as the most moving the critic had ever seen, brought out the humour in the barbed exchange with Antonio and Bassanio in Act I, Scene iii: rather than as 'a heavy, sober figure . . . I played the first scene in a very jovial, laughing way but at the same time shrewdly doing business'.[40] Both saw Shylock's scene with Jessica, Act II, Scene v, as 'Shylock's most private scene', where for once 'there is no need for a public face' before potential enemies, but also as deeply problematical while at the same time being essential to establish Shylock's motivation. Suchet found it 'the most difficult scene of the play', since nothing in it overtly justified Jessica's statement 'Our house is hell' (II. iii. 2): the domestic scene between Shylock and Jessica thus 'leaves open the whole question of Jessica's subsequent behaviour' and creates further problems of interpretation and the balance of sympathies in the play.[41] Stewart, who found this scene 'the very heart of the play' and 'the scene that consistently gave me the greatest satisfaction', saw it as indicative of a household devoid of warmth and affection. His Shylock was 'a man deeply unhappy and embittered, a man from whom life had been removed. And therefore Jessica was a creature who could give him no love, nor could he return it.'[42] The production underlined this point by having Shylock strike Jessica hard, in a graphic illustration of how life in that household was hell.

In rehearsing Act III, Scene i, both Stewart and Suchet were initially 'inhibited' and puzzled by 'Hath not a Jew eyes?', feeling dissatisfied with the traditional reading of this famous speech. In Stewart's words: 'In rehearsals ... I stumbled unhappily through that quicksand of famous lines, memories of other actors' voices and rhythms in my head, and what proved to be a mistaken notion of what the speech was about: injustice, compassion, racial tolerance, equality and the evils of bad example.'[43] Both were wary of playing the speech as 'an appeal for pathos', with Shylock in effect saying 'I am a poor wronged fellow' and thus sentimentalizing the role. Instead, Suchet played the speech to emphasize Shylock's 'deep anger', and Stewart as 'a vigorous justification of revenge', which could be seen as 'calculating, cold-blooded', and bitter. Both actors saw the exchange with Tubal in the later part of Act III, Scene i as important in explaining Shylock's motivation, but the two productions differed from nearly all others in playing Tubal as 'dispassionate, detached and in the end disapproving'.[44] From this point on, in both performances, Shylock is implacable in his pursuit of revenge: 'from then on, it's going to be kill ... There is then no doubt at all that he is going to go right the way through with it'.[45]

A further difference between the two productions was the unusual approach Sinead Cusack took to the role of Portia in 1981, in which she found 'distinctly tragic' overtones. Both productions directed by Barton brought out the drama and suspense in the trial scene, with a Shylock fully convinced of the justice of his cause and, in 1981, a Portia who 'gives him opportunity after opportunity to relent and to exercise his humanity'.[46] The two actors played Shylock's final exit very differently, with Stewart 'humiliating himself and crawling', relieved that half his property had been restored and therefore anxious 'to get away with as much as he could', avoiding further punishment, whereas Suchet emphasized the pathos of Shylock's situation, bringing out 'the simplicity of the lines' Shakespeare gives him, speaking the words 'I am content' (IV. i. 389) with calm resignation.[47] The two productions agreed in attempting to 'restore an equal balance between Bassanio,

35

Shylock and Portia', finding a thematic unity in the Venice and Belmont scenes: one reviewer commented on the 'evenness' of the 1978–9 production as a great virtue, praising the way the cast functioned as an ensemble, rather than allowing the play to become 'Shylock and Company'.[48]

Two productions of the 1980s took the risk of presenting an exaggeratedly semitic and histrionically bloodthirsty Shylock (almost a reversion to Macklin's conception of the role) and an unsympathetic Portia. Both productions caused offence in the way they foregrounded the issues of anti-Semitism, and both received mixed reviews. In John Caird's 1984 production, featuring spectacular, obtrusive sets, Ian McDiarmid played Shylock 'as Jewish as I can make him', in flowing robes, ringlets, and guttural speech, and Frances Tomelty's Portia was described by various reviewers as strong-willed, hard-driven, and condescending.[49] Where this production received generally unfavourable notices, Antony Sher's Shylock, in Bill Alexander's 1987 production, again for the RSC, occasioned violent disagreement among critics. I loathed the production, walking out at the interval (my view, or something like it, was shared by the *Observer* and *Daily Telegraph* critics); and yet the *Independent* reviewer could call the central performance 'an outright triumph, a sensational piece of acting which leaves one awed and intoxicated', and the *Sunday Times* reviewer 'watched it with shuddering admiration'.[50] One thing on which the critics agreed was that the production was a one-man show, dominated by its central performance ('just as it used to in old-fashioned theatre', one critic remarked), with the other parts generally undercast and under-rehearsed. Another critic remarked that the 'dry and bloodless' Belmont scenes almost seemed 'irrelevant' to the main business.[51] Portia was abrasive, disdainful, and bossy, Bassanio was a rabid anti-Semite and an unabashed fortune-hunter. It may be that, as Bulman suggests, the director's intention was to portray a Belmont no less materialistic and bigoted than Venice, but the Belmont scenes in production were insufficiently realized, making the play seem 'fatally lopsided'.[52]

What was distinctive about this production was that it openly sought to offend and disturb, evoking racial stereotypes: the actor and director 'encouraged audiences on a visceral level to loathe Shylock', seeking 'to play on bourgeois audiences' intolerance of racial differences'.[53] Sher's Shylock was as unassimilated, as visibly foreign, as anyone could possibly be: indeed, in his Near Eastern robes, turban, long beard, and heavy Levantine accent, he resembled the popular image of an Arab terrorist. This is Shylock as terrifying Other, a creature out of nightmares, the blood-libel come to life. Reports of the trial scene (which I did not see, having fled the theatre before that) suggest that it was played to extract the most possible terror and suspense, with a Shylock fully capable of butchering Antonio in open court.

In the production design, there was a great deal of visual symbolism, with much play with the Star of David and the cross, liturgical or Hebrew chanting to betoken human sacrifice or crucifixion. The Christians, without exception, were depicted as blatantly and offensively anti-Semitic ('a bunch of Venetian fascists', in one review), expressing their hostility by choral shouts of 'Jew, Jew' and by an extraordinary amount of spitting, stone throwing, and physical abuse, with Salerio and Solanio at one point wrestling Shylock to the ground and prodding him with a stick. The keynote of this production, illustrated in over-explicit detail, was 'The villainy you teach me I will execute, and it shall go hard but I shall better the instruction' (III. i. 65–6). Hate begets hate, violence begets violence: as Sher said in an interview, pointing out explicit contemporary analogies to the Middle East and his native South Africa, 'the more violent is the segregation and racism, the more bloody will be the revenge'.[54] The intention of the production seems to have been, in a form of Brechtian alienation, to force members of the audience to recognize their complicity with oppression, thus leading them to question their own unexamined racism. Sher himself pointed out the difficulties inherent in this approach: 'The problem with this production, which seeks to point out racism, is that we may appeal in exactly the wrong way to any racists in the audience . . . Often, in the trial scene, when the tables are turned on me, there's a roar of delighted applause . . . It's like being at a Nazi rally.'[55]

Another aspect of this production was its unusual emphasis on overt homosexuality among the Venetians. Salerio and Solanio were a squabbling gay couple, and Antonio and

Bassanio kept fondling one another, even in the trial scene, exchanging a passionate kiss at the end of Act I, Scene i. The overall effect was not so much to establish a rivalry between Antonio and Portia for the love of Bassanio (a reading advanced by a number of recent critics) as to present a closed subculture in which same-sex liaisons were the norm. Perhaps here again the production intended to challenge homophobic assumptions in the audience, but the effect was miscalculated, succeeding only in annoying many of the reviewers (Bulman cites fifteen references in the reviews).[56]

Three other productions sought to reinterpret the play in various ways. David Thacker's 1993–4 RSC production opted for modernization, with David Calder's Shylock a civilized and elegant City businessman and the Venetians yuppie stock-market traders in Margaret Thatcher's Britain. The updating, emphasizing themes of greed and hypocrisy, worked well in the first part of the play, but reviewers commented that the transformation of Shylock into an implacable avenger was not made fully credible, and the Belmont scenes, as in several other productions, were rather pallid. Peter Hall's 1989 West End production, with Dustin Hoffman as Shylock, seems in contrast to have been intended as a 'straight' production, with no attempts to update or make an ideological point. Unusually, Hoffman made 'Suff'rance is the badge of all our tribe' (I. iii. 105) the keynote of his performance, giving a performance 'stronger on irony than passion',[57] emphasizing the character's quick-witted survival skills in a society where he had long experienced casual anti-Semitism. The Venetians tended to be under-characterized, though in this production they came across as more likeable than in most recent versions of the play. The Globe production, directed by Richard Olivier in 1998, featured a strong, intelligent performance of Portia by Kathryn Podgson, convincing in her male disguise, and by far the funniest and most inventive Launcelot Gobbo I have ever seen in the Italian *commedia dell'arte* clown Marcello Magni.[58] Shylock was played by the German actor Norbert Kentrup, grave, imposing, and dignified, plainly the moral and intellectual superior of his Venetian adversaries; his heavy German accent underlined his status as alien, but made some of his lines hard to follow. The performance of other roles was very uneven, with several actors who did not have the faintest idea of how to speak Shakespearian blank verse.

Trevor Nunn's National Theatre production of 1999, initially seen in the intimate surroundings of the Cottesloe and then restaged for the larger Olivier theatre, was widely acclaimed, with Henry Goodman's Shylock praised as 'one of the great interpretations ... searing and devastating', showing 'enormous range' and sensitivity to detail. This production was explictly conceived as a post-Holocaust *Merchant*, set in the Europe of the late 1920s or early 1930s, a 'period when anti-Semitic thought and anti-Semitic behaviour [were] becoming current and even ... voguish', fuelled by 'the dangerous attraction to nationalism'.[59] The depiction of a decadent café society, with echoes of *Cabaret* and Weimar Germany, grounded the play in a recognizable social milieu, and the Venetians, never caricatured, were nicely differentiated, with David Bamber's anxious, middle-aged provincial Antonio nearly as much of an outsider as Shylock. To me, the one discordant note was an ill-advised attempt to make Launcelot Gobbo a stand-up comedian, providing entertainment to the crowd of Venetian idlers. Goodman, drawing on his childhood memories of being chased by anti-Semitic mobs in the East End, presented a Shylock who was constantly aware of his Jewish identity, and no other production I have ever seen gave such a strong and convincing sense of a Jewish community from which Shylock drew sustenance. Tubal and Jessica played unusually prominent roles, and there were interpolated bits of dialogue in which Shylock and Jessica addressed one another in Yiddish. As Michael Billington commented in his review,[60] the production effectively contrasted 'Christian hedonism' with 'Hebraic faith'.

Goodman's Shylock, a complex and multifaceted figure, was presented as 'a mass of enlightening contradictions'.[61] As in John Barton's two productions, the domestic scene with Jessica and Launcelot Gobbo within Shylock's 'sober house' (II. v. 36) was given unusual weight in establishing Shylock's motivation. Goodman's Shylock is an overprotective father, whose house is not hell but stifling for a Jessica, soberly dressed and kept behind closed doors (like Gilda in *Rigoletto*), who blossoms sexually, visibly altering in appearance, once the restraint is removed. Like Stewart, Goodman slaps Jessica near the end of the scene, but here it is a gesture of impotent, cloying love, immediately prompting remorse. Nunn gave the play a new ending, with Jessica, who had wept uncontrollably at 'I am never merry when I hear sweet music' (v. i. 69), standing apart, bereft, singing a Yiddish song she had previously sung with her father, as a lament for the home to which she could never return. To add a further ominous note, Nunn moved Portia's line 'It is almost morning', preceded by 'This night methinks is but the daylight sick' (v. i. 124–5, 295), to serve as a kind of coda, accompanied by sounds of thunder (an allusion perhaps to the end of *The Cherry Orchard*).

Though Shylock and Portia have only one scene together, their 'very strong theatrical relationship' is central to the trial scene (where they are, in Sinead Cusack's words, 'head and shoulders above the rest of the group' and set apart from the other characters on stage) and to the play as a whole. The problem with the role of Portia, as Cusack remarked, is how 'to reconcile the girl at home in Belmont early in the play with the one who plays a Daniel come to judgement in the Venetian court'. In their very different performances, Cusack in 1981 and Derbhle Crotty in 1999, the two outstanding Portias in recent productions, presented a Portia who changed during the action of the play: according to Cusack, 'both Bassanio and Portia grow wiser and more mature in the course of the play, and particularly in the casket "trial"'.[62] Where Cusack in the opening scenes brought out the seriousness of Portia's predicament as 'a living daughter curb'd by the will of a dead father' (I. ii. 24–5), Crotty was bored, brittle, rather prickly, unawakened. Nunn's production, even more than Barton's, treats the casket scene (Act III, Scene ii) as setting a test for Portia as well as Bassanio. More than in any production I have seen, Crotty makes Portia's assumption of a male identity in the trial scene the unlocking of hidden potential. Slightly gauche, looking like a very bright but inexperienced young lawyer arguing her first big case, Crotty's Portia, with her cropped hair and horn-rimmed glasses, is convincingly androgynous. In this production, Portia and Shylock are worthy adversaries, powerfully arguing for what each believes passionately to be right. When Goodman's Shylock says to the Duke 'What judgment shall I dread doing no wrong?' (IV. i. 89), he is not playing verbal games but claiming, in all sincerity, that what he seeks is not revenge but justice, as servant of the law. The debate between justice and mercy is embodied in the two antagonists, so that the 'quality of mercy' speech is not a set piece, a succession of famous lines worn smooth by endless repetition, but a logical response to Shylock's 'On what compulsion must I? tell me that' (IV. i. 179).

In a characteristic directorial touch, at a key point of the trial scene, when Shylock, knife in hand, appears irrevocably set on killing Antonio, Tubal (played as Shylock's loyal and sympathetic friend and as representative of the community of Venetian Jews) looks at Shylock reproachfully and then silently leaves the courtroom. Goodman's Shylock, not implacable as in the traditional reading, hesitates and wavers, torn by inner conflict, even as he approaches Antonio with the knife, keeping the audience in suspense to the last moment. In Cusack's interpretation of the role, Portia came to the trial scene with a plan clearly worked out in advance: 'when I entered the courtroom I knew exactly how to save Antonio; my cousin had shown me that loophole in the law which would save him from the bond'.[63] Crotty, in contrast, played 'Tarry a little, there is something else' (IV. i. 301) as desperate improvisation, thinking on her feet, with Portia turning over leaves of heavy law volumes in search of a precedent that might serve to deflect the revenger's knife, turning Shylock's insistence on the strict letter of the law against him:

> This bond doth give thee here no jot of blood,
> The words expressly are 'a pound of flesh'.

> (IV. i. 302–3)

One reviewer described the trial scene in this production as 'morally harrowing',[64] a phrase that nicely described the intellectual and visceral excitement that Nunn's *Merchant* generated.

III

Any performance of a play as complex and problematical as *The Merchant of Venice* is necessarily an interpretation of the play, a contribution to critical debate. Though the text of a play cannot be conceived of as 'totally malleable', subject to any passing whim of a critic or director, nevertheless, as Jonathan Miller has said, in initially approaching a play, especially one as familiar as *Merchant*, it can be useful to treat it as 'premises to be let that are to be occupied by persons as yet unknown'. 'It seems to me that it is precisely because subsequent performances of Shakespeare's plays are interpretations, rather than copies, that they have survived. The amplitude of Shakespeare's imagination admits so many possible interpretations that his work has enjoyed an extraordinary afterlife unforeseeable by the author at the time of writing.'[65]

No modern production of *The Merchant of Venice* has followed the example of Granville's *The Jew of Venice* or Stoll's 1927 essay in treating Shylock as a comic character. The closest approximation was the expressionist production by the Russian director Theodore Komisarjevsky in 1932 at the Shakespeare Memorial Theatre at Stratford, which treated the play as 'a gorgeous fairy-story', with cubist sets, surrealist costumes, and frequent allusions to *Alice in Wonderland* and to *commedia dell'arte*. The director consciously sought to 'scale Shylock down to . . . size', avoiding what he considered false pathos and playing the trial scene as grotesque farce, but the production's satiric treatment of bourgeois decadence still made Shylock more victim than villain.[66] No production in recent years has taken the line of the Danson–Coghill reading of the play as Christian allegory, fashionable in the 1970s, celebrating the triumph of Christian mercy over the Old Law; indeed, Trevor Nunn's 1999 production contrasted Jewish sobriety with the frivolousness and hypocrisy of nominal Christians.

In Hitler's Germany, *The Merchant of Venice*, with a grotesque and monstrous Shylock, wholly unsympathetic, was used as material for Nazi propaganda in several productions.[67] Anti-Semitic stereotypes were consciously evoked with ironic intent in Bill Alexander's 1987 production, with Antony Sher playing Shylock as 'provocatively offensive' in his behaviour and appearance.[68] Except for Sher, most recent Shylocks have chosen to present him not as a monster, terrifying in his malevolence, but as a complex and multifaceted figure: in

David Suchet's interpretation, for example, 'the audience . . .
can form their own ideas about him. Sometimes they will hate
him, sometimes like him, or laugh at him or feel sympathy
with him.'[69] Productions have differed in conceiving of Shylock
as visibly, even defiantly alien (Sher, McDiarmid, Kentrup,
Mitchell) or as, initially at least, seeking integration into
Venetian society (Olivier, Calder, Stewart, Hoffman). 'I would
be friends with you and have your love' (I. iii. 134) is
susceptible of a wide variety of interpretations along the
spectrum of irony and sincerity. Productions have differed as
to whether Shylock was intent on revenge against Antonio
from the beginning of the play or sought revenge on the
Venetians only after Jessica had eloped with Lorenzo; since
Olivier, most Shylocks have favoured the latter reading, giving
particular emphasis to Shylock's grief at his daughter's desertion. Despite their differing approaches to the part, Olivier,
Stewart, Suchet, Calder, and Goodman all made the exchange
with Tubal in the latter part of Act III, Scene i, and especially
the lines 'I had it of Leah when I was a bachelor: I would not
have given it for a wilderness of monkeys' (III. i. 111–13) central
to their interpretation.

A number of modern productions have sought to bring out
Shylock's domestic side, treating his 'sober house' as a refuge
and his command to 'stop my house's ears' (II. v. 34–6) as an
attempt to ward off the dangerous influences of Venetian
society, where other productions have treated Shylock as a
thoroughgoing materialist in a society given over to the
worship of Mammon. Productions have differed greatly in the
extent to which they see Venice and Belmont as embodying
opposed values or as essentially similar. Those interpretations
that, like the productions of Miller in 1970, David Thacker in
1993–4, or the German director Peter Zadek with the Berliner
Ensemble in the 1995 Edinburgh festival, use the play to mount
a sustained critique of 'the corrosive cash nexus', tend to treat
Shylock as 'largely indistinguishable' from 'his Gentile fellow-
operators on the Rialto'[70] and to minimize distinctions between
Venice and Belmont. In many ways, the most difficult problem
for any interpreter is the play's generic instability, its uneasy
mixture of elements reminiscent of tragedy and of traditional
comedy: as Ruth Nevo has put it, 'the vividly realized, specific

motivation of betrayal, bereavement and revenge . . . forecloses comic possibilities by actualizing the very human harm, the human suffering, which comedy exists to circumvent'.[71] The 1999 National Theatre production is among the very few I have seen that has been sufficiently attentive to the delicate balance between Venice and Belmont, and avoids falling into the trap of making the return to Belmont in Act V seem anticlimactic or jarringly inconsistent with what has gone before.

Fig. 1. Henry Irving as Shylock, in the famous Victorian production, Lyceum, 1879. Irving continued to play Shylock for forty years.

Fig. 2. Venetian street scene, Charles Kean production, Princess's Theatre, 1858. The son of Edmund Kean, Charles Kean was famous for the elaborate pictorial nature of his sets, with 'authentic' Venetian detail. Irving used a similar set for the interpolated scene of Shylock's return.

Fig. 3. Laurence Olivier as Shylock, Jeremy Brett as Bassanio, National Theatre, 1970, directed by Jonathan Miller. The production was set in the Victorian period, with an assimilated, dignified Shylock.

Fig. 4. Laurence Olivier as Shylock, National Theatre, 1970.

Fig. 5. Patrick Stewart as a down-at-heel, miserly Shylock, Avril Carson as Jessica, Royal Shakespeare Company, 1978, directed by John Barton.

Fig. 6. Sinead Cusack as an anxious Portia, 'distinctly tragic', Terry Wood as a formidable Prince of Morocco, Royal Shakespeare Company, 1981, directed by John Barton.

Fig. 7. Henry Goodman as Shylock, Derbhle Crotty as Portia, National Theatre, 1999, directed by Trevor Nunn.

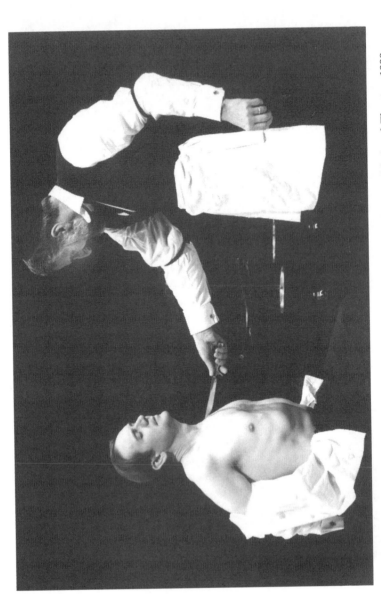

Fig. 8. Henry Goodman as Shylock, David Bamber as Antonio, trial scene, National Theatre, 1999, directed by Trevor Nunn.

3

'O that I were a man!'

I

In certain respects, the action of several Shakespeare comedies, in which the heroine dresses in man's clothes in pursuit of one or another goal, can be seen as an extension of Beatrice's reiterated complaint in *Much Ado about Nothing*, 'O that I were a man!' (*Much Ado*, IV. i. 302). When Beatrice says this, in the scene with Benedick immediately following the public shaming and rejection of her cousin Hero, she is saying, in anger and frustration, that men are privileged and empowered in ways that women are not: 'O that I were a man! What, bear her in hand until they come to take hands, and then with public accusation, uncovered slander, unmitigated rancour – O God that I were a man! I would eat his heart in the market-place' (*Much Ado*, IV. i. 302–6). Evidence of such inequality has been provided in the first half of Act IV, Scene i, where Hero is not allowed to speak up for herself and is condemned on very flimsy evidence, subjected to a cruel tongue lashing and physical violence by her fiancée and her father. All the men on stage except for Benedick and Friar Francis immediately line up against her, retreating behind male chauvinist assumptions: that all women are whores, that daughters and wives are disposable property belonging to men, that women who transgress are damaged goods bringing shame on their husbands and fathers.

> CLAUDIO. There, Leonato, take her back again.
> Give not this rotten orange to your friend;
> She's but the sign and semblance of her honour.
> .   .   .   .   .   .
> DON PEDRO. I stand dishonour'd, that have gone about

45

> To link my dear friend to a common stale.
> LEONATO. ·   ·   ·   ·   ·   ·
> Why ever wast thou lovely in my eyes?
> Why had I not with charitable hand
> Took up a beggar's issue at my gates,
> Who smirched thus, and mir'd with infamy,
> I might have said, 'No part of it is mine;
> This shame derives itself from unknown loins'?
>
> (*Much Ado*, IV. i. 302, 64–5, 130–5)

Men, as Beatrice puts it in this scene, wear swords (Benedick had a moment earlier sworn, 'By my sword, Beatrice, thou lovest me'), and can defend their honour in a duel or in physical combat: this, of course, is exactly what Benedick does later in the play, when, breaking with his former friends because of their treatment of Hero, he challenges Claudio to a duel. Beatrice is by custom prevented from wielding the phallic sword; but her tongue is her sword, enabling her to defend herself with verbal wit and, a skilled rhetorician redefining the key terms of 'manhood' and 'valour', to secure a male champion who can act on her behalf.

> O that I were a man for his sake, or that I had any friend would be a man for my sake! But manhood is melted into curtsies, valour into compliment, and men are only turned into tongue, and trim ones too: he is now as valiant as Hercules that only tells a lie and swears it. I cannot be a man with wishing, therefore I will die a woman with grieving. (*Much Ado*, IV. i. 316–23)

Portia in *The Merchant of Venice* and Rosalind in *As You Like It* both dress in men's clothes and are empowered by their new identity. Viola in *Twelfth Night*, who in the guise of Cesario actually wears a sword but does not know how to use it ('A little thing would make me tell them how much I lack of a man' (III. iv. 307–9)), finds her male disguise a constant source of embarassment, involving her in difficulties and opening up possibilities that, if she had worn female dress, would not exist. She may lack the 'little thing' that would identify her as male (the penis, again equated with the sword – or, in *The Merchant of Venice*, 'the young clerk's pen' (V. i. 237)), but in the action of the play Viola, like Portia and Rosalind, is simultaneously male and female.

> VIOLA. I am the man: if it be so, as 'tis,

Poor lady, she were better love a dream.

. . . .

What will become of this? As I am man,
My state is desperate for my master's love:
As I am woman (now alas the day!)
What thriftless sighs shall poor Olivia breathe?

(*Twelfth Night*, II. ii. 24–5, 35–8)

Portia makes the same bawdy joke about an anatomical 'lack' in discussing with Nerissa the plan to 'turn to men' (III, iv. 60–2, 78), and a variant of the conceit ('addition' rather than lack – 'adding one thing to my purpose nothing') is central to the depiction of the Fair Youth as 'master mistress of my passion' (lines 2, 11–12) in sonnet 20.

With Portia, Rosalind, and Viola the double or divided identity conferred on them by cross-dressing is consistently described as androgynous rather than, even in outward show, unequivocally masculine. In each of the plays the heroine is 'accoutered like' and appears to be a youth or adolescent rather than a mature man, and such passages as the following, from *The Merchant of Venice*, can serve to evoke a further impersonation beyond girl-as-boy in reminding the Elizabethan audience that a boy actor is playing the role:

> POR.   I'll hold thee any wager
> When we are both accoutered like young men,
> I'll prove the prettier fellow of the two,
> And wear my dagger with the braver grace,
> And speak between the change of man and boy,
> With a reed voice, and turn two mincing steps
> Into a manly stride.
>
> (III. iv. 62–8)

Both Malvolio and Orsino comment on the youth Cesario's apparent status as not-quite-man or androgyne, one of them slightingly and one with an admiration that foreshadows the ultimate resolution of the Viola–Olivia–Orsino love triangle, once Viola is able to don 'other habits', which will enable her to play 'a woman's part' (V. i. 386).

> MALVOLIO. Not yet old enough for a man, nor young enough for a boy: as a squash is before 'tis a peascod, or a codling when 'tis almost an apple. 'Tis with him in standing water, between boy

47

and man . . . One would think his mother's milk were scarce out
of him.

(I. v. 158–64)

> ORSINO. For they shall yet belie thy happy years,
>   That say thou art a man. Diana's lip
>   Is not more smooth and rubious: thy small pipe
>   Is as the maiden's organ, shrill and sound,
>   And all is semblative a woman's part.

(I. iv. 30–4)

Critics disagree in the emphasis they place on a presumed
awareness in the Elizabethan audience that the women portrayed on stage – Portia, Rosalind, Viola (and for that matter,
Desdemona, Lady Macbeth, and Cleopatra) – are really boys.
Lisa Jardine in *Still Harping on Daughters* has argued that the
appeal of cross-dressing is in part erotic, aimed at kindling
homosexual desire in the male members of the audience,
claiming 'that these figures are sexually enticing *qua* transves-
tied boys, and that the plays encourage the audience to view
them as such'.[1] My own view is closer to that argued by
Catherine Belsey and Stephen Orgel: that the convention of
theatrical cross-dressing tends to 'destabilize the categories
and question what it means to be a man or a woman', to
disrupt traditional binary assumptions of fixed gender and
gender roles.[2] When Viola in *Twelfth Night*, in a riddling speech
the meaning of which is inaccessible to Orsino (and partly to
Viola herself) but not to the audience, says 'I am all the
daughters of my father's house, | And all the brothers too' (II.
iv. 121–2), she is both man and woman: as Belsey says, the
speaker of the riddle 'occupies a place which is not precisely
masculine or feminine'.[3] Theatrical illusion, on the Elizabethan
stage, as in drama generally, induces its audience, by a
suspension of disbelief, to feel that the actors embody, or
during the time of representation actually become, the characters they are playing, so that we do not look behind the
character to the person playing the role. It is always possible
for a dramatist consciously to break the illusion, for an actor to
speak *as actor* to the audience, stepping outside his or her role,
as Rosalind does ('if I were a woman . . .') in the epilogue to
As You Like It, or as Puck does ('Give me your hands, if we be

48

friends . . .') inviting applause at the end of *A Midsummer Night's Dream*.

A convention of the Elizabethan stage is that the disguise of the cross-dressed heroine is impenetrable to the other characters, except for those explicitly made aware of her secret identity. With Portia and Nerissa, Rosalind and Celia, and Viola, all the male characters they encounter in disguise are fooled by the impersonation: indeed, in the trial scene of *The Merchant of Venice*, if any of the characters other than Nerissa were aware that Balthazar was really Portia, the scene would lose much of its effectiveness. As Belsey says, 'Portia's right to exercise her authority depends on her lawyer's robes, and the episode can be seen as making visible the injustice which allows women authority only on condition that they seem to be men'.[4] Portia says things as Balthazar that she could never conceivably have had the opportunity to say as Portia: in this sense at least, the disguise as a young doctor of Rome is enabling, conferring on Portia freedom from the constraints of custom. In one of the few comic moments in the tense dramatic confrontation of the trial scene, Portia directs a barbed comment to Bassanio, with some of the riddling ambiguity of Viola's 'I am all the daughters of my father's house,/ And all the brothers too':

> POR. Your wife would give you little thanks for that
> If she were by to hear you make the offer.

(IV. i. 284–5)

Portia, without breaking the decorum of her disguise, speaks both as a woman and as a man, both is and is not present in the Venetian courtroom. In Act V, when the characters return to Belmont, the action is based on the ignorance of the two husbands, Bassanio and Gratiano, that their wives have not been waiting patiently for them at home, but have been leading active lives in Venice, engaged in 'work' that their husbands 'know not of' (III. iv. 57–8). As we will see, the comic elements in the scene involve an unstated contest for mastery, in which the wives play on their husbands' fear that their wives have been unfaithful (compounded by the husbands' guilt at having broken a solemn vow). Because of the superior knowledge conveyed by the costume they have been able to assume – a quasi-magical ability to see their husbands and not be seen by them – Portia and Nerissa are in control, and can challenge conventional assumptions about what men and women are permitted or expected to do:

> POR. I will become as liberal as you,
> I'll not deny him any thing I have,
> No, not my body, nor my husband's bed.
>
> (v. i. 226–8)

Portia's pun on 'double' sums up the destabilizing, disruptive tone of the exchange: 'In both my eyes he doubly sees himself | . . . swear by your double self' (v. i. 244–6). Portia is 'double' in her identity, simultaneously male and female, free agent and faithful wife; Bassanio is 'double' as deceitful, self-divided, unreliable.

Feminist critics have disagreed as to whether the traditional ending of Shakespearian romantic comedy, where the heroine, abandoning her 'masculine usurp'd attire' and resuming her 'maiden weeds' (*Twelfth Night*, v. i. 248, 253), is reintegrated into the community in marriage or betrothal, is intrinsically conservative. The licence of carnival, it is argued, is always temporary, and the patriarchal order is reinscribed when play-time comes to an end:

> 'Jack shall have Jill,
> Nought shall go ill;
> The man shall have his mare again, and all shall be well.
>
> (*Midsummer Night's Dream*, III. ii. 461–3)

In the words of Clara Claiborne Park:

> The temporary nature of the male disguise is of course essential, since the very nature of Shakespearean comedy is to affirm that disruption is temporary, that what has turned topsy-turvy will be restored. It is evident that Rosalind has enjoyed the flexibility and freedom of the masculine role, but it is also evident that she will gladly and voluntarily relinquish it . . . Brilliant and fascinating women are a pleasure to watch, once we can be sure they will accept the control even of the Bassanios and Orlandos of the world.[5]

Other critics have argued that cross-dressing in *As You Like It* and *The Merchant of Venice* offers a greater challenge to assumptions of male hegemony, that the energies unleashed cannot be easily contained, the possibilities of free agency closed off. Rosalind, in her disguise as Ganymede, is master of the revels in the Forest of Arden, stage-managing the action, and Portia, similarly privileged by her male dress and by knowing things unavailable to the other characters, is able to assume a position of authority in Venice that she does not relinquish on her return to Belmont. At the very least, the cross-dressed heroine in *As You Like It*, *The Merchant of Venice*, and *Twelfth Night* is afforded the opportunity 'to redefine . . . the position of women in a patriarchal society' to her own advantage, and thus to expose fantasies of male dominance and control to be without solid foundation: 'Even while it reaffirms patriarchy, the tradition of female transvestism challenges it precisely by unsettling the categories which legitimate it.'[6]

Those critics who argue versions of the containment thesis (the view that 'tends simply to assign to patriarchy the absolute power it claimed for itself and to ignore the possibilities for women's resistance') admit that *The Merchant of Venice* is a special case.[7] It does not end with a marriage; instead, the wedding of Portia and Bassanio takes place (offstage) in Act III, Scene ii, and any celebration is interrupted by the news of the forfeiture of the bond and Antonio's impending death.

> POR. First go with me to church, and call me wife,
> And then away to Venice to your friend:
> For never shall you lie by Portia's side
> With an unquiet soul . . .
> .   .   .   .   .   .
> My maid Nerissa, and myself meantime
> Will live as maids and widows; – come away!
> For you shall hence upon your wedding day.
>
> (III. ii. 302–10)

Portia's equivocation in saying that she and Nerissa 'will live as maids and widows' in their husbands' absence is characteristic of this part of the play, in which, during the interval between wedding ceremony and consummation, the relationship between husband and wife is renegotiated. Portia and Nerissa may live in enforced chastity, cut off from their husbands' embraces, but they do not spend their time, like Viola's imaginary sister, sitting 'like Patience on a monument, | Smiling at grief' (*Twelfth Night*, II. iv. 115–16). Instead, they commit themselves to active intervention in a sphere of activities normally not open to women. As 'learned woman' in the trial scene, Lisa Jardine has argued, Portia is an ambivalent figure: 'The legal knowledge she deploys to save Antonio modulates Portia's initial obedient conformity with the patriarchal demands on her, in her position as female heir, into something close to unruliness.'[8] When Portia pledges herself in marriage to Bassanio, she makes the vow conditional, and thus imposes a further test on Bassanio:

> This house, these servants, and this same myself
> Are yours, – my lord's! – I give them with this ring,
> Which when you part from, lose, or give away,
> Let it presage the ruin of your love,
> And be my vantage to exclaim on you.

> (III. ii. 170–4)

II

At the beginning of the play, Portia's freedom of action is severely restricted. Her opening line is 'By my troth, my little body is aweary of this great world' (I. ii. 1–2): critics have often pointed out the parallel with Antonio's 'In sooth I know not why I am so sad', the first line of the play. Nerissa attempts to cheer her up, telling her of the 'abundance' of her 'good fortunes' as a wealthy heiress – 'a lady richly left', in Bassanio's phrase, and a valued prize to her many 'renowned suitors' – and as mistress of a large household (I. i. 161, 169; I. ii. 4). In the casket scene, Portia describes the advantages of her situation to Bassanio, in the moment of relinquishing them:

> But now I was the lord
> Of this fair mansion, master of my servants,
> Queen o'er myself.

> (III. ii. 167–9)

As heiress, not subject to the control of any living male relative, she is in a more fortunate position than Viola, Rosalind, or

Celia (her situation is in some ways close to that of Olivia, who has the additional advantage of the title of Countess). Yet this apparent freedom is illusory, since she is bound by the will of her dead father, exercising an absolute authority over her from beyond the grave, which denies her the right to choose a husband for herself, or even to refuse one she finds antipathetic, and leaves her feeling impotent and frustrated: 'The brain may devise laws for the blood, but a hot temper leaps o'er a cold decree' (I. ii. 17–19). In the 1981 National Theatre production, Sinead Cusack in this scene emphasized Portia's melancholy and her sense of being trapped. 'O me the word "choose"! I may neither choose who I would, nor refuse who I dislike, so is the will of a living daughter curb'd by the will of a dead father: is it not hard Nerissa, that I cannot choose one, nor refuse none?' (I. ii. 22–6). Portia's initial situation, then, is precisely that of women in a traditional patriarchal and patrilineal society, passed like a parcel from the ownership of her father to that of her husband, treated as a material object and not as desiring subject, in order to provide legal safeguards for the ownership of the paternal estate.

The will of Portia's father is not legally binding in the same way as Antonio's bond with Shylock, in that it depends on voluntary compliance. Each of the suitors must agree to bind himself to the terms of the will, and Portia too must agree, out of a sense of filial duty and respect, not to 'refuse to perform [her] father's will' (I. ii. 89). As she tells Morocco, the first of the three suitors who tries to solve the riddle of the caskets:

> You must take your chance,
> And either not attempt to choose at all,
> Or swear before you choose, if you choose wrong
> Never to speak to lady afterward
> In way of marriage.

(II. i. 38–42)

Nerissa tries to assure Portia that her father's intentions were benevolent and that he was not acting as tyrant or ignoring his daughter's welfare in setting up a lottery, the winner of which gains her as prize. But her claim that the victor will automatically be someone Portia 'shall rightly love' (can love? will come to love? ought to love? will already love?) is far from convincing, particularly in view of the descriptions of patently unworthy suitors that follow. 'Your father was ever virtuous, and holy men at their death have good inspirations, – therefore the lott'ry that he hath devised in these three chests of gold, silver, and lead, whereof who chooses his meaning chooses you, will no doubt never be chosen by any rightly, but one you shall rightly love.' (I. ii. 26–32). A lottery is ruled at least partly by chance, and skill in puzzle solving is no guarantee of compatibility in marriage. The badinage of Portia and Nerissa in this scene suggests some anxiety over Portia's enforced passivity: what if the wrong person, a fool or a brute or a pompous ass, should choose the right casket?

> NER. How like you the young German, the Duke of Saxony's nephew?
> POR. Very vildly in the morning when he is sober, and most vildly in the afternoon when he is drunk: when he is best, he is a little worse than a man, and when he is worst he is little better than a beast – and the worst fall that ever should fall, I hope I shall make shift to go without him.
> NER. If he should offer to choose, and choose the right casket, you should refuse to perform your father's will, if you should refuse to accept him.
> POR. Therefore for fear of the worst, I pray thee set a deep glass of Rhenish wine on the contrary casket.
>
> (I. ii. 80–92)

Like Beatrice, who at the beginning of *Much Ado* is far more in control over her own destiny and has already exercised her right of refusal several times ('Let him be a handsome fellow, or else make another curtsy and say, "Father, as it please me"' (*Much Ado*, II. i. 50–2)), Portia in this scene displays her independent spirit and impatience of restraint by her caustic wit, used as a weapon in her defence. But at the end of this scene, she announces her intent to 'die as chaste as Diana, unless I be obtained by the manner of my father's will' (I. ii. 102–4), and in the casket scene with Bassanio, after wavering for a moment – since he is the man I want, why not bend the rules a bit? – Portia decides to adhere to the conditions laid down by her father, and to allow Bassanio a free choice, which might, under the rules of the game, unite or sever them:

> I pray you tarry, pause a day or two
> Before you hazard, for in choosing wrong
> I lose your company; therefore forbear a while.
> .   .   .   .   .   .
>   I could teach you
> How to choose right, but then I am forsworn,
> So will I never be, – so may you miss me, –
> But if you do, you'll make me wish a sin,
> That I had been forsworn. Beshrew your eyes,
> That have o'erlook'd me and divided me.
>
> (III. ii. 1–3, 10–15)

Some critics have argued that Portia directs Bassanio's choice in the casket scene, giving broad hints in a song about the instability of appearances, in which the first three lines end with rhymes on 'lead'. In Jonathan Miller's 1970 production, the scene was played as broad farce, with Portia blatantly assisting her favoured candidate, and such critics as Moody and Fiedler have argued that 'Portia provides her lover with the clue he needs to find her' and that, given his faults of character, it is 'quite unbelievable' that Bassanio 'should have chosen it unprompted'.[9] A more common view, which I share, is that 'the idea that Portia tips off Bassanio' is inconsistent with 'the expectations . . . aroused by the dramatic and literary conventions the play exploits' and with the overall structure of a play in which the casket scene is 'one in a series of trials' taking place in Belmont or in Venice.[10] As Sinead Cusack has said, commenting on the 1981 production: 'We decided early in rehearsal that neither Portia nor Nerissa knew the contents of the caskets . . . Early in rehearsal I discounted, as too cheap and trite on either Shakespeare's or Portia's part, the idea that the three rhymes ("bred", "head", "nourished") invited the fourth rhyme "lead".'[11]

The conventions of fairy tale are that the third lover in a sequence will free the imprisoned princess from enchantment, after the first two suitors have failed, and that, in keeping with the deceptiveness of 'outward shows' (III. ii. 73), the un-regarded youngest son (or in the Cinderella story, the third daughter), seemingly a failure in the eyes of the world, will emerge triumphant. To play his destined role and fulfil the pattern, Bassanio must pass the test that has been set for him and choose rightly. As Auden says, in his illuminating commentary on the casket motif:

> In the fairy-tale world, what appear to be the personal choices of the characters are really the strategic choices of the storyteller, for within the tale the future is predestined. We watch Portia's suitors choosing their casket, but we know in advance that Morocco and Arragon cannot choose the right one and that Bassanio cannot choose the wrong one, and we know this, not only from what we know of their characters but also from their ordinal position in a series, for the fairy-tale world is ruled by magic numbers.[12]

In *Il Pecorone*, Shakespeare's principal source, there is no moral element in the test (and no father setting the conditions): here the hero himself makes two unsuccessful attempts, tricked by the lady, and in the third he outwits her. Bassanio's test, in contrast, is a test of character involving the solution of a riddle.

The same test, involving the same riddle, is set for each of the suitors who agrees to the conditions. The Prince of Morocco is presented as an attractive suitor, a valiant warrior and by no means a fool. Portia, addressing him respectfully as 'renowned prince', declares to him that, in comparison with other suitors (none of whom has had the courage to undergo the test of the caskets), she views him favourably:

> Your self (renowned prince) then stood as fair
> As any comer I have look'd on yet
> For my affection.
>
> (II. i. 20–2)

Several critics, including Fiedler, have worried over Portia's alleged racism in 'Let all of his complexion choose me so' (II. vii. 79), as at variance with these lines and with the evident plea for racial tolerance in Morocco's earlier 'Mistake me not for my complexion, | The shadow'd livery of the burnish'd sun' (II. i. 1–2). Fiedler sees the line as characteristic of Portia's disdain (and, he suggests, that of the Elizabethan audience) for the 'upstart alien', as shown in her witty, dismissive comments on national types – the drunken German, the foppish Frenchman, the horse-mad Neopolitan – in Act I, Scene ii, and considers the Moorish prince 'to represent the absolute pole of otherness' in the play.[13] But on the evidence of the text,

Morocco is a plausible candidate for Portia's hand, a warrior prince who, like Othello and Tamburlaine, has proved himself in battle, and who can state confidently that he is her equal 'in birth . . . in fortunes . . . and in qualities of breeding' (II. vii. 32–3). His exotic, foreign origin makes him more, not less, eligible as a suitor, and illustrates the way in which princes from 'all the world', 'the four corners of the earth', as far away as 'the vasty wilds of wide Arabia', have come in pursuit of Portia (II. vii. 38–43). What leads him to choose wrongly, rejecting the leaden casket out of hand, on the grounds that 'a golden mind stoops not to shows of dross', is excessive pride in his own accomplishments and reputation, leading him to equate his own 'value', his 'deserving', with his 'estimation' in the eyes of the world (II. vii. 20, 25–30). Like Arragon and unlike Bassanio, he 'takes his own desert for granted',[14] and, led astray by false appearance, is blind to the sinister implications of the inscription 'what many men desire' on the golden casket. As the casket, once it is opened, tells him, 'All that glisters is not gold' and a tempting 'outside' may deceive: Morocco may be 'bold', but he is far from 'wise . . . in judgment' (II. vii. 5, 65–71).

Arragon, another foreign prince, is less attractive, with his flaws in character and moral obtuseness more immediately apparent. Every production I have seen has sought to bring out the comic aspects of Act III, Scene ix, treating Arragon as smug, vain, with a grotesquely inflated sense of his own dignity and importance. Arragon is a snob, who places an absurdly high valuation on the 'estates, degrees, and offices' conferred by aristocratic birth, contemptuous of 'the fool multitude' whom he equates with 'low peasantry' (II. ix. 26, 41, 46).

> I will not choose what many men desire,
> Because I will not jump with common spirits,
> And rank me with the barbarous multitudes.
>
> (II. ix. 31–3)

Sublimely egotistical and narcissistic, he scarcely mentions Portia in his lengthy speech justifying his choice, in which he unwittingly reveals his unworthiness. Since no one can ever 'assume desert', Arragon is incapable of making the right choice, and is shown his true image in 'the portrait of a blinking idiot' (II. ix. 51, 54).

Bassanio's choice of the leaden casket may be predetermined by the dramatic pattern, but he still needs to free himself from the worldly values he has shown himself in earlier scenes to share with the other suitors. Like all the suitors, he is initially attracted by Portia's great wealth and her status as a valued prize, the 'golden fleece' for which 'many Jasons come in quest' (I. i. 170–2). We also learn in the opening scene that, by being 'too prodigal' in living beyond his means, he is heavily in debt, having 'disabled [his] estate', and that, an instinctive gambler, he is willing to take the 'hazard' of borrowing still more money in the hope that, by securing a rich heiress, he can 'get clear of all the debts' he owes (I. i. 122–34, 151). In Geary's crisp, no-nonsense statement of his initial situation, 'Bassanio, unable to manage his financial affairs efficiently, needs money, and the easiest and quickest way to get it is by finding himself a rich wife'.[15] Though some critics have interpreted Bassanio's profligacy as indicative of a generosity of spirit, a 'willingness to give and hazard' in the 'willing, generous and prosperous transactions of love's wealth',[16] Bassanio, as we see him in Acts I and II, does not appear to differ appreciably from his fellow Venetians in his attitudes and values. Shylock, describing to Launcelot Gobbo the difference between his old and new master, sees Bassanio as a typical 'prodigal Christian', inclined to 'waste | His borrowed purse' in 'feasting' and in 'shallow foppery' (II. v. 15, 35–7, 49–50). Yet all the Venetians are materialists, trading in goods, money, or credit. Where Shylock saves and accumulates capital, the Christian Venetians, engaged in 'merchandise' of various kinds, spend their money freely, as they invest it in more risky 'ventures' that may or may not pay off (I. i. 40–5). When Bassanio suggests to his more cautious friend Antonio that he should 'hazard' a further loan, 'shoot another arrow that self way | That you did shoot the first', he is, as a venture capitalist, making a business proposition, as well as appealing to Antonio's friendship (I. i. 148–51). In the world of *The Merchant of Venice*, 'economic and moral conduct'[17] are not always easy to reconcile.

What Shakespeare needs to do in the scene where Bassanio makes his choice of the caskets is to 'prepare the audience to accept Bassanio as a suitor worthy of Portia'.[18] He does this partly by inserting a lengthy exchange between Portia and Bassanio at the beginning of Act III, Scene ii, in which the two confess their love, with Portia, not wanting to lose Bassanio if he chooses wrongly, urging him to delay his choice: 'I would detain you here some month or two | Before you venture for me' (III. ii. 9–10). The initial exchange emphasizes Portia's forced inactivity, as she must passively look on – 'I stand for sacrifice' (III. ii. 57) – hoping that Bassanio will pass the test set by her father, but unable to influence the outcome:

> Live thou, I live – with much much more dismay,
> I view the fight, than those that mak'st the fray.
>
> (III. ii. 61–2)

Bassanio emerges victorious because he is the only one of the suitors able to see beyond appearances, recognizing the possibility of a standard of valuation other than the calculation of gain and loss and the 'hope of fair advantages' (II. vii. 19). The other suitors think only of themselves, none of them willing to 'give and hazard all he hath', and only Bassanio realizes that a riddle must be difficult, embodying ambiguities, and does not give up its meaning at first glance.

> So may the outward shows be least themselves, –
> The world is still deceiv'd with ornament.
> .   .   .   .   .   .
> There is no vice so simple, but assumes
> Some mark of virtue on his outward parts.
>
> (III. ii. 73–4, 81–2)

Suspicious of the 'seeming truth' with which 'cunning' is able 'to entrap the wisest' (III. ii. 100–1), Bassanio ignores the inscriptions to investigate the hidden meaning of the caskets themselves and the substances of which they are made, gold, silver, and 'meagre' lead. A gambler to the end, he chooses that which on the surface is least attractive and least promising:

> But thou, thou meagre lead
> Which rather threaten'st than dost promise aught,
> Thy paleness moves me more than eloquence.
>
> (III. ii. 104–6)

When Portia addresses Bassanio as victor in the contest for her hand (responding to his courteous request that his good fortune be 'confirm'd, seal'd, ratified' by her), the metaphors she uses, surprisingly, are those of accountancy, as she draws up a balance sheet or inventory. Marriage is presented here as a business transaction, transferring property under contract.

> You see me Lord Bassanio where I stand,
> Such as I am; though for myself alone
> I would not be ambitious in my wish
> To wish myself much better, yet for you,
> I would be trebled twenty times myself,
> A thousand times more fair, ten thousand times more rich,
> That only to stand high in your account,
> I might in virtues, beauties, livings, friends
> Exceed account: but the full sum of me
> Is sum of something: which to term in gross,
> Is an unlesson'd girl, unschool'd, unpractised,
> Happy in this, she is not yet so old
> But she may learn: happier than this,
> She is not bred so dull but she can learn.
>
> (III. ii. 148–62)

Here Portia seems to be speaking with her father's voice, in exaggerated terms of humility and subservience, unable to express that which might 'exceed account' other than in monetary terms. In a play notoriously problematical in its ideology, this speech seems particularly indigestible, and has proved an embarrassment to feminist critics. Though a critic like Brown who idealizes Belmont can present the speech, sunnily, as 'Portia's modest, eager, rich-hearted committal to Bassanio',[19] it is hard to disagree with Lisa Jardine's caustic observation that in this speech the 'inventory of Portia's womanly deficiencies contradicts everything that the rest of the play explicitly tells us about her'.[20] Quite explicitly, Portia's speech affirms a conservative, hierarchical view of marriage in which the man is sovereign lord and the woman passive, obedient subject. The lines that follow those quoted above are ideologically indistinguishable from Katherina's speech at the end of *The Taming of the Shrew* ('Thy husband is thy lord, thy life, thy keeper, | Thy head, thy sovereign . . .' (v. ii. 147–8)), affirming her acquiescence 'in a rigidly defined hierarchy of male power and privilege',[21] surrendering all legal rights to the property that was once hers and accepting the new role of chattel.

> Happiest of all, is that her gentle spirit
> Commits itself to yours to be directed,
> As from her lord, her governor, her king.
> Myself, and what is mine, to you and yours
> Is now converted. But now I was the lord
> Of this fair mansion, master of my servants,
> Queen o'er myself: and even now, but now,
> This house, these servants, and this same myself
> Are yours, – my lord's!
>
> (III. ii. 163–71)

Jardine sees this passage as embodying 'the ambivalent attitudes circulating in the play', 'a confused cultural response' toward the learned, active, or resourceful woman in texts of the early modern period.[22] But the final lines of Portia's speech suggest something rather different from the pervasiveness of patriarchal values. Where the equivalent speech in *The Taming of the Shrew* ends with Katherina's symbolically placing her hand beneath her husband's foot as token of submission, Portia, using contractual language, imposes a new set of conditions on Bassanio, to which Bassanio immediately consents:

> POR.   I give them with this ring,
>   Which when you part from, lose, or give away,
>   Let it presage the ruin of your love,
>   And be my vantage to exclaim on you.
>   .   .   .   .   .   .
> BAS.   But when this ring
> Parts from this finger, then parts life from hence, –
> O then be bold to say Bassanio's dead!
>
> (III. ii. 171–4, 183–5)

Much of the later action of the play is prefigured in Portia's gift of the ring and the quasi-magical symbolic value she attributes to it (rather like Othello's handkerchief, woven with magic in the web) as token of mutual trust and continued love. Having passed the test of the caskets successfully, Bassanio is faced with a further difficult choice, in having to decide between the rival claims of his wife and his dearest friend.

III

If there is rivalry between Portia and Antonio, it is not manifested by overt jealousy on either part. Antonio behaves generously in unhesitatingly advancing money (to the 'uttermost' of his capacity, he says twice (I. i. 156, 181)) to his friend, before even hearing details of Bassanio's venture.

> You know me well, and herein spend but time
> To wind about my love with circumstance,
> And out of doubt you do me now more wrong
> In making question of my uttermost
> Than if you had made waste of all I have:
> Then do but say to me what I should do
> That in your knowledge may by me be done,
> And I am prest unto it: therefore speak.
>
> (I. i. 153–60)

Portia in her turn, as soon as she hears the news of Antonio's misfortune, is no less extravagantly generous in her response: again, all her resources are at Bassanio's disposal. In neither case is there any element of calculation of profit or advantage. Aware at all times of her wealth and social position, Portia can afford to subscribe to an aristocratic ideal of generosity.

> POR. What sum owes he the Jew?
> BAS. For me three thousand ducats.
> POR.   What no more?
>   Pay him six thousand, and deface the bond:
>   Double six thousand, and then treble that,
>   Before a friend of this description
>   Shall lose a hair through Bassanio's fault.
>   .   .   .   .   .   .
>   You shall have gold
> To pay the petty debt twenty times over.
>
> (III. ii. 296–301, 305–6)

Such critics as Barber and Danson tend to idealize the unstinting 'bounty' (III. iv. 9) of Portia and Antonio as indicative of a joyous spirit of festivity or of total selflessness, in contrast with a Shylock whose motto is 'Fast bind, fast find' (II. v. 53) and who loathes music and feasting. Yet in offering large sums of money to the spendthrift Bassanio (described by

Auden as 'one of those people whose attitude toward money is that of a child; it will somehow always appear by magic when really needed'), Antonio and Portia, if not buying love with money, are seeking to express love through the gift of money.[23] As Bassanio makes explicit in addressing Antonio as one to whom 'I owe the most in money and in love' (I. i. 131), a gift necessarily implies obligation, places the receiver emotionally as well as financially in the debt of the giver.

Love and friendship in Renaissance texts can be seen as wholly compatible or, more frequently, as potentially in conflict. In the brief scene before Portia's departure to Venice in male disguise, she uses neoplatonic imagery to suggest that she must necessarily love Antonio (whom she has never met) because he is likely to be 'virtually identical in inward and outward form'[24] with Bassanio, whom she loves. If A loves B and B loves C, then A must love C: the proposition is flawed logically, and, as the later action of the play demonstrates, does not hold up under pressure.

> in companions
> . . . . . .
> Whose souls do bear an egall yoke of love,
> There must be needs a like proportion
> Of lineaments, of manners, and of spirit;
> Which makes me think that this Antonio
> Being the bosom lover of my lord,
> Must needs be like my lord. If it be so,
> How little is the cost I have bestowed
> In purchasing the semblance of my soul
> From out the state of hellish cruelty!
>
> (III, iv. 11–21)

Antonio's letter to Bassanio, read out at the end of the previous scene, presents the love between the two male friends as decidedly unequal, with some doubt on Antonio's part whether Bassanio will bother to turn up for his funeral. The seeds of conflict are sown in a letter that, coming immediately after the trial of the caskets, asks Bassanio again to choose: which of us do you love more, your old and dear friend or the new wife I bought for you, at the risk of my life? In its melancholy and somewhat lachrymose tone, Antonio's letter resembles his later 'I am a tainted wether of the flock, | Meetest for death' (IV. i. 114–15). He welcomes death and sees no possibility of escaping punishment: 'My bond to the Jew is forfeit, and (since in paying it, it is impossible I should live), all debts are clear'd between you and I, if I might but see you at my death: notwithstanding, use your pleasure, – if your love do not persuade you to come, let not my letter.' (III. ii. 315–20).

A number of critics, starting with Midgley and Auden in the 1960s, have seen Antonio as 'a man whose emotional life . . . is concentrated upon a member of his own sex'.[25] Most recent productions have followed this line in presenting Antonio as a latent or 'unconscious homosexual' doting on Bassanio[26] or even, in some cases, as overtly effeminate or camp in his manner, expressing his love for Bassanio by kissing or fondling him at every opportunity.[27] I would argue instead that the unequal relationship between Antonio and Bassanio is a homosocial bond of friendship in which the erotic content is implicit and not overt, rather like that between the Poet and the Fair Youth in the sonnets.

> But since she pricked thee out for women's pleasure,
> Mine be thy love, and thy love's use their treasure.
>
> (sonnet 20, ll. 13–14)

Implicit in Antonio's moving farewell to his bosom friend Bassanio, when he faces imminent death, 'arm'd and well prepar'd' (IV. i. 260), is the assumption that the love between men and women, capable of being expressed physically ('thy love's use'), is inferior to the love between two male friends, where such physical expression is neither expected nor desired.

> Commend me to your honourable wife,
> Tell her the process of Antonio's end,
> Say how I lov'd you, speak me fair in death:
> And when the tale is told, bid her be judge
> Whether Bassanio had not once a love.
>
> (IV. i. 269–73)

When Bassanio immediately agrees with this comparative judgement, not only elevating the love of comrades above marriage but blithely announcing his willingness to 'sacrifice' both wife and marriage to save Antonio (IV. i. 278–83), the potential conflict between Portia and Antonio is made overt. The two disguised women, Portia and Nerissa, both comment with some asperity on the readiness of the husbands to barter away their wives.

> NER. 'Tis well you offer it behind her back,
> The wish would make else an unquiet house.
>
> (IV. i. 289–90)

Later in this scene, after Bassanio initially resists the request of the disguised Portia to surrender the ring and violate his earlier vow, Antonio's intervention 'makes the contest perfectly explicit'[28] in setting the claims of marriage and friendship directly in opposition. Bassanio chooses again, and this time he fails to pass the test set by Portia.

> ANT. My Lord Bassanio, let him have the ring,
> Let his deservings and my love withal
> Be valued 'gainst your wife's commandment.
>
> (IV. i. 445–7)

The strategies that the cross-dressed Portia adopts, first in saving Antonio from the threat posed by Shylock and then, in the comic contentions of Act V, in securing her own marriage from the competing bonds and obligations of friendship, will be discussed in the next two chapters.

4

'I stand for judgment'

Most recent productions of *The Merchant of Venice* have presented Jessica's desertion of her father's household and religion as a central motivating factor prompting Shylock's revenge against his enemies. The tradition begins with Irving's celebrated Victorian production, which includes an interpolated scene depicting Shylock's return to his deserted house, and has persisted, with varying emphases, in productions directed by Jonathan Miller, John Barton, and Trevor Nunn, among others.[1] Such an interpretation is compatible with a sympathetic or unsympathetic treatment of Jessica, the runaway bride and Christian convert who admits to being 'ashamed to be my father's child' (II. iii. 17). In their badinage in Act V, Jessica and Lorenzo openly construe her flight as theft, equating (as Shylock does) the loss of material goods with the loss of a daughter:

> LOR.   In such a night
> Did Jessica steal from the wealthy Jew,
> And with an unthrift love did run from Venice,
> As far as Belmont.
>
> (V. i. 14–17)

The same paradoxical association of 'unthrift love' with calculation of material advantage is found in the scene of the flight itself, where the emphasis on the casket, full of jewels and ducats 'worth the pains', as visible signs of this 'exchange' (II. vi. 33–5), serves a similar function to the pun on 'steal':

JES. I will make fast the doors and gild myself
With some moe ducats, and be with you straight.

(II. vi. 49–50)

Shylock's violent reaction to the loss of his ducats and his daughter in the scene with Tubal makes an explicit link between the injury he feels himself to have suffered and his equally immoderate desire for revenge. Henry Goodman, in the recent National Theatre production, gave a particular emphasis to 'I never felt it till now': in this interpretation, pain or humiliation suffered becomes the immediate cause of pain inflicted in retribution, providing a form of emotional release.

> SHY. The curse never fell upon our nation till now, I never felt it till now ... loss upon loss! the thief gone with so much, and so much to find the thief, and no satisfaction, no revenge, nor no ill luck stirring but what lights o' my shoulders, no sighs but o' my breathing, no tears but o' my shedding.
> TUB. Yes, other men have ill luck too, – Antonio (as I heard in Genoa) –
> SHY. What, what, what? ill luck, ill luck?
> TUB. – hath an argosy cast away coming from Tripolis.
> SHY. I thank God, I thank God! is it true, is it true?
>
> (III. i. 77–9, 84–93)

In the earlier part of the scene, where Shylock is taunted by the callous Venetians Solanio and Salerio, his mordant conclusion 'The villainy you teach me I will execute' (III. i. 65) can be read as directed at Christian Venice in general, rather than as indicating a clearly worked-out plan of revenge on Antonio. At that point in the scene, Shylock does not yet know that Antonio's 'ill luck' with trading ventures has afforded him an opportunity for revenge on someone who, he thinks, has sought consistently, with deliberate malice, to do him injury: 'he hath disgrac'd me, and hinder'd me half a million, laugh'd at my losses, mock'd at my gains, scorned my nation, thwarted my bargains, cool'd my friends, heated mine enemies' (III. i. 48–52). Throughout the scene with Tubal, Shylock oscillates between two powerful emotions, pain at the loss of his daughter and hatred of Antonio. The close proximity of 'I'll plague him, I'll torture him' and 'thou torturest me Tubal' (III.

67

ii. 106–7, 110) makes the association between pain felt and pain inflicted quite explicit.

In recent years, Jessica and Lorenzo have had a generally bad press with critics. Sigurd Burckhardt's summary judgement is representative:

> As lovers, Jessica and Lorenzo stand in the sharpest imaginable contrast to Portia and Bassanio. Their love is lawless, financed by theft and engineered through a gross breach of trust. It is subjected to no test: 'Here, catch this casket, it is worth the pains', Jessica says to Lorenzo to underscore the difference. The ring which ought to seal their love is traded for a monkey. They are spendthrift rather than liberal, thoughtless squanderers of stolen substance.[2]

The condemnation of Jessica on moral grounds for selfishness and 'parasitical self-indulgence' is even stronger in Quiller-Couch's introduction to the 1926 New Cambridge edition: 'Jessica is bad and disloyal, unfilial, a thief; frivolous, greedy, without any more conscience than a cat and without even a cat's redeeming love of home. Quite without heart ... she betrays her father to be a light-of-lucre carefully weighted with her sire's ducats ... Shylock is intolerably wronged.'[3] Several recent productions have treated Jessica more sympathetically, presenting the domestic environment of Shylock's household as oppressive, a prison from which Jessica, starved of love, seeks the first opportunity to escape. The 1999 National Theatre production, with an overprotective rather than cold and unfeeling Shylock, was particularly sensitive in its use of costume, as Jessica casts off her drab, sober outer garments, discovering the ambiguous joys of sexuality in the unaccustomed freedom of Belmont. The pointed comic exchanges of the clown Launcelot Gobbo and Jessica in Act III, Scene v – 'he tells me flatly there's no mercy for me in heaven, because I am a Jew's daughter' (III. v. 29–30) – touch on uncomfortable topics: whether converts from Judaism will be damned or saved, whether Jessica is by nature or inclination her father's daughter, and whether the motive for conversion is anything more than material advancement.

Like Portia's father, Shylock treats his daughter as a valuable possession, something to be guarded. The 1999 production brought out the extent to which, as a Jew in a Christian society,

Shylock made his house a citadel and sanctuary, seeking to 'stop my house's ears, I mean my casements' (II. v. 34) from the intrusive sounds and sights of Christian Venice. With Jessica's defection, it has been argued, 'a blow is struck at all that Shylock holds dear, his pride of race, the sober decency of his household life and the dear sanctity of the family and family bonds'.[4] Among religious Jews, even today, a child marrying out of the faith is considered dead, and pictures of that child are destroyed or turned to the wall as a token of apostacy or betrayal. Nearly all modern productions of the play have, in presenting the scene with Tubal, placed particular emphasis on the symbolic sundering of familial bonds – an insult not only to the father, but to the dead mother – in Jessica's purchase of a monkey with a family heirloom, her mother's ring.

> TUB. One of them showed me a ring that he had of your daughter for a monkey.
> SHY. Out upon her! – thou torturest me Tubal, – it was my turquoise, I had it of Leah when I was a bachelor: I would not have given it for a wilderness of monkeys.
>
> (III. i. 108–13)

At Shylock's next appearance after the scene with his fellow Jew Tubal, in Act III, Scene iii, he has seemingly been transformed into an implacable instrument of revenge, a killing machine, refusing to be deflected from his chosen course. He is obdurate in rejecting Antonio's pleas (indeed, all that Antonio can manage to say to him is 'Hear me yet ... I pray thee hear me speak'), contemptuously dismissing all claims of human sympathy, charity, or mercy (III. iii. 3, 11).

> SHY. I'll have my bond. I will not hear thee speak,
> I'll have my bond, and therefore speak no more.
> I'll not be made a soft and dull-eyed fool,
> To shake the head, relent, and sigh, and yield
> To Christian intercessors: follow not, –
> I'll have no speaking, I will have my bond.
>
> (III. iii. 12–17)

Rather than entering into any dialogue with Antonio, he repeats the same phrase three times, as an assertion of will and an absolute refusal to admit even the possibility of compromise. This refusal, Shylock says here and in the trial scene, is grounded on a sacred oath: he is implicitly claiming divine sanction for his obduracy, casting himself as defender of a rigorous divine law, the observance of which overrides any prudential considerations.

> I have sworn an oath, that I will have my bond:
> Thou call'st me dog before thou hadst a cause,
> But since I am a dog, beware my fangs, –
> The duke shall grant me justice.
>
> (III. iii. 5–8)

> I have possess'd your grace of what I purpose,
> And by our holy Sabbath I have sworn
> To have the due and forfeit of my bond, –
> If you deny it, let the danger light
> Upon your charter and your city's freedom!
>
> (IV. i. 35–9)

It is striking that, except for 'beware my fangs', Shylock in Act III, Scene iii never speaks of revenge on Antonio or of the hatred he bears him: it is left to Antonio, after Shylock's exit, to comment on Shylock's motivation and on the anterior relationship between the two men. Instead, Shylock invokes justice, the laws of the Venetian state, the sacredness of oaths, and the fulfilment of contracts.

The issues more fully explored in the trial scene are set out in the brief, unpleasant encounter between Antonio and Shylock in Act III, Scene iii, in which the claims of mercy and justice are shown to be difficult to reconcile. Shylock's opening words, calling on the gaoler as visible embodiment of the punitive power of the state, are 'Gaoler, look to him, – tell not me of mercy' (III. iii. 1). Mercy, the central term in Portia's eloquent appeal to Shylock in the trial scene, is characterized by Shylock here as weakness, culpable folly in a market society where each competitor seeks an edge over his rivals. And yet his vocabulary, like Portia's later, is implicitly theological, contrasting the Old Testament and the New. 'Christian inter-cessors' may literally refer to Venetian Christians who seek to intercede on Antonio's behalf, but the phrase inevitably recalls the doctrine of the incarnation and the Sermon on the Mount, with its critique of Old Testament morality.

Ye have heard that it hath been said, An eye for an eye, and a tooth for a tooth. But I say to you, That ye resist not evil: but whosoever shall smite thee on the right cheek, turn to him the other also . . .

Ye have heard that it hath been said, Thou shalt love thy neighbour, and hate thine enemy. But I say unto you, Love your enemies, bless them that curse you, do good unto them that hate you, and pray for them which despitefully use you, and persecute you.   (Matt. 5: 38–9, 43–4)

Unlike his friends Solanio and Gratiano, who see Shylock as less than human, a 'wolvish . . . ravenous' beast ('It is the most impenetrable cur | That ever kept with man'; 'O be thou damn'd, inexecrable dog!' (III. iii. 18–19; IV. i. 128, 138)), Antonio is fully aware of the human motivation underlying Shylock's antipathy towards him. Resolute for death and ready to pay his 'bloody creditor' the debt demanded (III. iii. 34), Antonio, like Shylock, subscribes to a competitive ethos in which, according to the tribal code, injuries must be avenged, an eye for an eye and a tooth for a tooth, and in which those outside the tribe are enemies, capable of seeking the life of those who have offended them.

> ANT. Let him alone,
> I'll follow him no more with bootless prayers.
> He seeks my life, his reason well I know;
> I oft deliver'd from his forfeitures
> Many that have at times made moan to me,
> Therefore he hates me.
>
> (III. iii. 19–24)

In an important exchange with Shylock, Antonio in effect concedes Shylock's later claim 'I stand for judgment' (IV. i. 103). He recognizes that, to all intents and purposes, Shylock has the law on his side, and that the case must be decided not in terms of the Duke's personal preferences, or by discretionary powers at the Duke's disposal, but in accordance with the laws of the Venetian state.

> SOL. I am sure the duke
> Will never grant this forfeiture to hold.
> ANT. The duke cannot deny the force of law:
> For the commodity that strangers have
> With us in Venice, if it be denied,
> Will much impeach the justice of the state,

71

> Since that the trade and profit of the city
> Consisteth of all nations.

(III. iii. 24–31)

I have discussed this passage in Chapter 1, commenting on its claim that Venetian justice is entirely impartial, treating citizens and strangers alike, and on its association of the laws of the state and property transactions. Shylock in the trial scene makes a similar point about Venetian law and the inviolability of contract, though more aggressively.

> The pound of flesh which I demand of him
> Is dearly bought, 'tis mine and I will have it;
> If you deny me, fie upon your law!
> There is no force in the decrees of Venice:
> I stand for judgment, – answer, shall I have it?

(IV. i. 99–103)

Presumably the pound of flesh is 'dearly bought' because it has in effect been purchased by the shame of Jessica's desertion, gilded with ducats, over and above the cash value of the 3,000 ducats that Antonio has failed to repay Shylock on the date stipulated in the bond. Portia makes the same pun in telling Bassanio 'Since you are dear bought, I will love you dear' (III. ii. 312).

Critics have often described Shylock as embodiment of the cash nexus, capable of reducing human beings to material objects to be bought and sold – one to whom 'a good man', with the term stripped of any moral connotations, is one whose financial resources are 'sufficient' to underwrite a business transaction (I. iii. 11–15). Barber, invoking Bergson's theory of the comic, sees Shylock as 'the ogre of money power' and antagonist of the festive comic spirit. 'Shylock . . . exhibits what should be human, degraded into mechanism. The reduction of life to mechanism goes with the miser's wary calculation, with the locking up, with the preoccupation of 'that which is mine own''.[5]

Where such critics as Barber, Danson, and Brown find in the play a thematic contrast of 'love and generosity', exemplified in Portia and Antonio, confronting and eventually defeating 'hatred and possessiveness',[6] other critics read the play's polarities of Venice and Belmont, Christian and Jew, in ironic

72

terms. René Girard, for example, sees a 'symmetry between the explicit venality of Shylock and the implicit venality of the other Venetians'.[7] Recent productions have tended to favour the ironic reading, emphasizing 'the essential likeness of Shylock and his judges'[8] in the trial scene. Shylock's speech to the court, defending his right to his property in the 'purchas'd' pound of flesh, in this interpretation, does not set forth his own values, reductive in their materialism, so much as expose the hypocrisy of nominal Christians who pretend to be ruled by a different set of values:

> You have among you many a purchas'd slave,
> Which (like your asses, and your dogs and mules)
> You use in abject and in slavish parts,
> Because you bought them, – shall I say to you,
> Let them be free, marry them to your heirs?
> Why sweat they under burthens? let their beds
> Be made as soft as yours, and let their palates
> Be season'd with such viands? you will answer
> "The slaves are ours", – so do I answer you.

(IV. i. 90–8)

Shylock is not of course inveighing against the evils of slavery: he is, with considerable polemical skill, telling his Christian judges that they have no moral right to accuse him of 'doing . . . wrong' (IV. i. 89) because in their everyday lives they behave exactly the way he behaves.[9] As in the 'Hath not a Jew eyes?' speech, enumerating the characteristics and faculties that Jews and Christians have in common, he is arguing that the same principles of self-interest animate Venetian aristocrat and money-lender: in this case, that both would prefer to be slave-owners rather than slaves.

The 'passion so confus'd' in Shylock when he discovers Jessica's flight, parodied mercilessly by Solanio – 'My daughter! O my ducats! O my daughter! | Fled with a Christian! O my Christian ducats!' (II. viii. 12, 15–16) – can be read as indicative of an inability to recognize any dimension beyond the material. Some critics have seen the scene with Tubal as comic, with Shylock 'a clear-cut butt . . . caught in compulsive, reflexive responses', though no production I have ever seen has taken this approach.[10] Wherever our sympathies may lie, the violence of Shylock's language in this scene contrasts sharply with the self-control he has shown earlier and will demonstrate in the trial scene: 'Two thousand ducats in that, and other precious, precious jewels; I would my daughter were dead at my foot, and the jewels in her ear: would she were hears'd at my foot, and the ducats in her coffin: no news of them? why so! and I know not what's spent in the search: why thou – loss upon loss!' (III. i. 79–84). In wishing and imagining Jessica dead, Shylock illustrates the narrow, permeable boundary separating love and hate, along with a conviction that his daughter, by crossing over to the enemy camp, has become his enemy, and a proper object for revenge: 'Hates any man the thing he would not kill?' (IV. i. 67)

Shylock's most famous speech, earlier in the scene, has also been subject to widely varying interpretations. Brown sees it as an attempt by Shylock 'to justify his murderous purpose' rather than as a 'plea for human tolerance', and Barber, similarly hostile to 'humanitarian' readings, finds Shylock's assertion of common humanity 'reductive' in its emphasis on 'the mechanism of stimulus and response'.[11] Patrick Stewart, who played Shylock in John Barton's 1978 production, saw the lines as a 'justification of revenge by Christian example', full of bitterness and anger: 'I began to pay attention to that word "revenge", appearing in the speech like a recurring major chord.'[12] Others have interpreted the speech as a direct challenge to the Venetians who deny any kinship with one they scorn as 'the dog Jew' (II. viii. 14) or 'the devil ... in the likeness of a Jew' (III. i. 19–20). Productions that emphasize the pervasive anti-Semitism of a smug and hypocritical Venetian society (for example, the 1970 and 1999 NT productions and the 1987 RSC production, very different in other respects) tend to interpret the speech not as an appeal for sympathy but as an indictment. Ryan, who finds in the speech 'an irrestistible egalitarian attitude' grounded in an evocation of 'the shared faculties and needs of our physical nature', sees 'the villainy you teach me I will execute' as the key statement in the speech and the fulcrum on which the later action turns. 'It explains that Shylock's bloodthirsty cruelty is not simply the result of the Venetians' abuse of him, but the deliberate mirror-image of their concealed real nature ... The revenge uncovers the hidden reality of a money-centred society, which has created Shylock in its own avaricious image.'[13]

The speech is prefaced by an exchange between Salerio and Shylock in which the Venetian remarks that, as *homo economicus*, Shylock can gain no material advantage from the pound of Antonio's flesh (Salerio uses the term 'good' here in much the same way as Shylock in the earlier scene with Bassanio). Shylock responds by enumerating, in practical, material terms, the ways in which Antonio has thwarted or injured him in a competitive market. The term 'revenge' begins and ends the passage, bracketing the series of rhetorical questions embodying a claim for recognition of common humanity.

> SAL. Why I am sure if he forfeit, thou wilt not take his flesh, – what's that good for?
> SHY. To bait fish withal, – if it will feed nothing else, it will feed my revenge; he hath disgrac'd me, and hind'red me half a million, laugh'd at my losses, mock'd at my gains, scorn'd my nation, thwarted my bargains, cooled my friends, heated mine enemies.
>
> (III. i. 45–52)

Though Stoll, Derek Cohen, and others have read the play as simple, unmediated expression of prevalent anti-Semitic prejudice (thus making Gratiano in the trial scene and Salerio and Solanio in this scene authorial spokesmen), it is difficult for modern readers or audiences to see the lines that follow as other than an attack on anti-Semitism.[14] Shylock's perspective here may be a partial one, but no production I have ever seen has treated these lines as self-serving rhetoric rather than as an appeal to brotherhood that the Christian Venetians have in their actions refused to recognize. Patrick Stewart, who was careful in his performance to guard against the 'sentimental interpretation of the role', made his Shylock representative of '*all* those oppressed and abused who stand up in the face of a hostile and powerful enemy ... not one Jew, but all victims who turn on their persecutors'.[15]

> And what's his reason? I am a Jew. Hath not a Jew eyes? hath not a Jew hands, organs, dimensions, senses, affections, passions? fed with the same food, hurt with the same weapons, subject to the

same diseases, healed by the same means, warmed and cooled by the same winter and summer as a Christian is? – if you prick us do we not bleed? if you tickle us do we not laugh? if you poison us do we not die? and if you wrong us shall we not revenge? – if we are like you in the rest, we will resemble you in that. (III. i. 52–62)

This eloquent passage changes direction halfway through, with the syntactical change from the repetition of 'same' (four successive clauses in parallel grammatical form, varied with doubling in a fifth) to a new pattern of four 'if' clauses (not conditional clauses so much as syllogistic cause and effect). This new set of rhetorical questions, distinctly aggressive in tone, re-establishes the binary distinction between 'you' and 'us' and, by implication, removes the voluntary element from the act of seeking revenge. The future tense in 'shall we not' or 'we will' might ordinarily introduce an element of uncertainty, predictions that may or may not be fulfilled, but the cumulative weight of the syntactical construction trumpets inevitability. Whatever may happen, you are responsible, and not I.

In the closing lines of the speech, Shylock disowns the stance of patient submission and 'humility' traditionally adopted by Jews in a hostile environment – 'Still have I borne it with a patient shrug, | For suff'rance is the badge of all our tribe' (I. iii. 104–5) – as well as the Christian ideals of meekness and forbearance, the 'better fortitude | Of patience and heroic martyrdom' later praised by Milton (*Paradise Lost*, IX, 31–2). 'Christian example' has taught him never to relax his guard, never to relent in seeking revenge on those who have wronged him. 'If a Jew wrong a Christian, what is his humility? revenge! If a Christian wrong a Jew, what should his sufferance be by Christian example? – why revenge! The villainy you teach me I will execute, and it shall go hard but I will better the instruction.' III. i. 62–6). If there is a declaration of brotherhood of Christian and Jew in these chilling lines, it is, as Koffler says, the 'brotherhood of fellow Christian cannibals, to whom all mankind is fodder'. In demanding payment of the pound of flesh, even if it means Antonio's death, Shylock, in this reading of the play, is exposing 'the hidden violence of the social order'.[16]

II

In the trial scene, Shylock mounts a similar challenge, refusing to make any concessions to Venetian authority or deviate from his chosen 'rigorous course' (IV. i. 8).

> By my soul I swear,
> There is no power in the tongue of man
> To alter me, – I stay here on my bond.

(IV. i. 236–8)

He declines to give reasons for his action, on the grounds that he is not required to do so, choosing to remain silent as to his motives. This refusal to plead (where, for example, like Brabantio in *Othello* he might have presented himself as an aggrieved father, or even given detailed arguments why the terms of the bond should be honoured exactly) is phrased in deliberately insulting terms, by implication denigrating not only Antonio but all Venetians.

> You'll ask me why I rather choose to have
> A weight of carrion flesh, than to receive
> Three thousand ducats: I'll not answer that!
> But say it is my humour, – is it answer'd?
> What if my house be troubled with a rat,
> And I be pleas'd to give ten thousand ducats
> To have it ban'd? what, are you answer'd yet?
> Some men there are love not a gaping pig!
> Some that are mad if they behold a cat!
> And others when the bagpipe sings i'th'nose
> Cannot contain their urine . . .
> .   .   .   .   .   .
> So can I give no reason, nor I will not,
> More than a lodg'd hate, and a certain loathing
> I bear Antonio, that I follow thus
> A losing suit against him! – are you answered?

(IV. i. 40–50, 59–62)

This brutally mechanistic and reductive account of human psychology may, as Barber suggests,[17] partly reflect Shylock's own unflattering and limited view of man as no better than a beast. But the gratuitously unpleasant imagery, as for over twenty lines he tells the Duke that he will not justify or explain

77

himself (my answer is that I will not answer), implicitly defies the authority of the court. As Johnson says, Shylock, 'being asked a question which the law does not require him to answer, stands upon his right', while, with conscious irony, giving 'such answers as he knows will aggravate the pain of the enquirer'.[18]

Antonio despairingly tells the Duke that any attempt to 'question with the Jew' is necessarily futile: Shylock will not play their game. The analogies Antonio uses, all from natural processes or phenomena, like Shylock's comparisons in the passage just quoted, rule out the element of volition, the possibility that one in a position of power might decide not to exercise that power in a cruel and arbitrary manner.

> I pray you think you question with the Jew, –
> You may as well go stand upon the beach
> And bid the main flood bate his usual height,
> You may as well use question with the wolf,
> Why he hath made the ewe bleat for the lamb:
>
>   .   .   .   .   .   .
>
> As seek to soften that – than which what's harder? –
> His Jewish heart!
>
> (IV. i. 70–4, 79–80)

These lines, like the later 'I am a tainted wether of the flock | Meetest for death' (IV. i. 113–14), may partly reflect a weary pessimism on Antonio's part, as with 'a masochistic and theatrical self-pity'[19] he welcomes death. The passage also increases suspense, making a tragic outcome seem likely, and thus helps tilt the sympathies of the audience towards the potential victim. But the lines also give expression to an anti-Semitism that Antonio shares with other Venetians: Shylock is hard-hearted *because* he is a Jew, all Jews are 'wolvish' beasts (IV. i. 138) with an appetite for blood.

Since the Duke is shown to share these views, his neutrality in the trial scene is open to question, and his impressive words addressed to Shylock, urging a 'gentle answer', are to say the least somewhat compromised, in the manner of Claudius' advice to Hamlet to follow the example of other courtiers and leave off his 'obstinate' mourning for his dead father (*Hamlet*, I. ii. 93). In the exchange between the Duke and Antonio that begins the trial scene, the Duke describes Shylock as

> A stony adversary, an inhuman wretch,
> Uncapable of pity, void, and empty
> From any dram of mercy.
>
> (IV. 1. 4–6)

The Duke's address when Shylock is called before the court is a formal public statement, setting forth the points at issue. Though the Duke uses honorific terms to evoke 'human gentleness' and 'tender courtesy' as against the 'apparent cruelty' in rigorously exacting the penalty, it is clear from his earlier remarks to Antonio that the Duke has no expectation that Shylock will accede to his request.

> Shylock the world thinks, and I think so too,
> That thou but leadest this fashion of thy malice
> To the last hour of act, and then 'tis thought
> Thou'lt show thy mercy and remorse more strange
> Than is thy strange apparent cruelty;
> And where thou now exacts the penalty,
> Which is a pound of this poor merchant's flesh,
> Thou wilt not only loose the forfeiture,
> But touch'd with human gentleness and love,
> Forgive a moiety of the principal,
> Glancing an eye of pity on his losses
> That have as late so huddled on his back,
> Enough to press a royal merchant down,
> And pluck commiseration of his state
> From brassy bosoms and rough hearts of flint,
> From stubborn Turks, and Tartars never train'd
> To offices of tender courtesy:
> We all expect a gentle answer Jew!
>
> (IV. i. 17–34)

Throughout the trial scene, Shylock is referred to as 'the Jew', and rarely by his name: twenty-two uses of 'Jew' (in direct address) or 'the Jew', as against only four of 'Shylock', two of which are part of the formal court procedure:

> POR. Which is the merchant here? and which the Jew?
> DUKE. Antonio and old Shylock, both stand forth.
> POR. Is your name Shylock?
> SHY.   Shylock is my name.
>
> (IV. i. 170–2)

79

The constant repetition of 'Jew', like the appeal to what 'the world thinks' at the outset of the Duke's speech, the evident sympathy for the Venetian 'royal merchant' bowed down by his trading losses, and the concluding pun on 'gentle/gentile' all serve to isolate the alien Shylock still further, reminding him he is not a Venetian. As in earlier references to Jessica as 'a gentle, and no Jew' (II. vi. 51), the assumption is that only those within the Christian communion can be gentle. The concluding lines of the Duke's speech construct Shylock as Tartar or Turk, rather in the way that Othello, another resident alien, feels compelled to disavow a 'malignant and a turbanned Turk' in himself to die as a Venetian (*Othello*, V. ii. 351–4).

A brief, emotionally charged exchange between Shylock and the Duke juxtaposes two incompatible moral principles, each taken by its proponent to be self-evidently true: as Coghill concedes, in an essay advancing a Christian allegorical reading of the play, 'the two principles for which . . . respectively they stand are both *inherently* right'.[20]

> DUKE. How shalt thou hope for mercy rend'ring none?
> SHY. What judgment shall I dread doing no wrong?
>
> (IV. i. 88–9)

The Duke's pointed question anticipates the argument of Portia's 'quality of mercy' speech and echoes the Christian injunction 'Judge not, that ye be not judged' (Matt. 7: 1). Though a subsidiary implication of the Duke's statement (since after all he is speaking as representative of secular authority, from the judge's chair) is that Shylock might at some point find himself on trial and would want to be treated mercifully, the main thrust of the line is theological. Shylock's answer, phrased as a rhetorical question, similarly associates human and divine justice, assuming that the latter underwrites the former. Because he is 'doing no wrong', acting in accordance with the law as strictly interpreted, he is not punishable by the law for his actions, and he need not fear divine punishment. Portia partly concedes the point that Shylock's actions appear to be compatible with Venetian law, and Shylock later asserts the primacy of divine law.

POR. Of a strange nature is the suit you follow,
Yet in such rule, that the Venetian law
Cannot impugn you as you do proceed.

(IV. i. 173–5)

SHY. An oath, an oath, I have an oath in heaven, –
Shall I lay perjury upon my soul?
No not for Venice.

(IV. i. 224–6)

In following 'a losing suit' (IV. i. 62) against Antonio, Shylock makes it clear throughout the trial scene that he is not motivated by considerations of profit and loss. Not only does he refuse payment of 3,000 ducats after the date when the bond is due, insisting that the bond is forfeit and the stipulated conditions must be met, but, in open court, he refuses the offer of twice the value of the bond (a usurious 100 per cent interest) and a later offer of three times the value of the bond.

SHY. If every ducat in six thousand ducats
Were in six parts, and every part a ducat,
I would not draw them, I would have my bond!

(IV. i. 85–7)

Instead Shylock, identifying his own cause with the strict construction of the law, argues that contracts must be enforced exactly as written: 'I stand here for law' (IV. i. 142); 'I crave the law' (IV. i. 202); 'I stay here on my bond' (IV. i. 238). As the legal historian Daniel Kornstein has pointed out, the argument for the supremacy of 'clear, precise, written law', in providing 'certainty and stability of contracts' and protection for potentially vulnerable individuals, has considerable validity: 'the apparent severity of a rigid but certain interpretation of law' is preferable to 'the discretion of a system that has already shown its bias'. Sir Edward Coke, defending the common law against the prerogative power of the Crown, argued, during the reign of James I, in favour of 'the golden and straight mete-wand of the law, and not the incertain and crooked cord of discretion'.[21] Portia endorses a similar position in the trial scene, and Shylock, not realizing the extent to which strict adherence to the letter of the law can prove disadvantageous to him, applauds the young doctor's words:

> POR. It must not be, there is no power in Venice
> Can alter a decree established:
> 'Twill be recorded for a precedent,
> And many an error by the same example
> Will rush into the state, – it cannot be.
> SHY. A Daniel come to judgment: yea a Daniel!
> O wise young judge how do I honour thee!

(IV. i. 214–20)

It has sometimes been argued that the conflict between justice and mercy in the trial scene reflects a distinction between two legal traditions in Elizabethan England. According to this view, *The Merchant of Venice* comments specifically on a topical issue in Shakespeare's day, 'a supposed conflict between the proponents of equity and the supporters of the common law', with Portia representing the concept of equity, as developed among the civil lawyers of the Court of Chancery, in opposition to 'the unreasonable rigour of the common law'. Such attempts to find in the play a close and systematic 'relationship to actual judicial practice' in Elizabethan England must necessarily lead to distortion, and can be shown to be historically inaccurate.[22] Though Portia urges Shylock 'to mitigate the justice of thy plea' (IV. i. 199), she is not proposing equitable relief from the conditions of the bond, but making a case for the exercise of mercy, using arguments that are theological rather than legal.

A second quasi-allegorical reading treats the play as 'Christian parable', with Shylock and Portia, Jew and Christian, representing the Old Law of strict observance, to be obeyed literally, and the New Testament doctrine of forgiveness of sins. According to Danson, the trial scene 'reveals the spirit of the law latent in its letter', resolving apparent conflict in 'a more comprehensive understanding of the nature of law, leading to its fulfillment both in justice and mercy'.[23] The problem with this extremely sunny, pietistic reading of the play is that it robs the trial scene of much of its emotional power, which depends on widening rather than narrowing the gap between justice and mercy. Portia's eloquent appeal in the 'quality of mercy' speech, seeking to show that mercy is both compatible with and superior to the 'sceptred sway' of earthly power, is summarily rejected by Shylock, who is ruled by a different set of imperatives.

82

Though the speech is often treated as a set piece suitable for declamation, detachable from its context, it responds directly to Shylock's line immediately before it, and to a brief exchange with Antonio, setting forth the facts of the case.

> POR. You stand within his danger, do you not?
> ANT. Ay, so he says.
> POR.   Do you confess the bond?
> ANT. I do.
> POR.   Then must the Jew be merciful.
> SHY. On what compulsion must I? tell me that.
>
> (IV. i. 176–9)

Portia, acting as mediator rather than advocate, uses 'must' to suggest logical consequence or non-enforceable moral obligation: given the conditions of the bond, the dispute could be resolved harmoniously if Shylock agreed voluntarily to be merciful. Shylock, who sees justice as punitive, interprets 'must' as compulsive: what power do you have to make me do so? His position here is the same as in the later 'Is it so nominated in the bond?' (IV. i. 255): the words of a contract must be enforced literally, with no scope for discretionary restraint. Portia responds by setting forth a different view of earthly power in a divinely ordered universe.

> The quality of mercy is not strain'd,
> It droppeth as the gentle rain from heaven
> Upon the place beneath: it is twice blest,
> It blesseth him that gives, and him that takes,
> 'Tis mightiest in the mightiest, it becomes
> The throned monarch better than his crown.
> His sceptre shows the force of temporal power,
> The attribute to awe and majesty,
> Wherein doth sit the dread and fear of kings:
> But mercy is above this sceptred sway,
> It is enthroned in the hearts of kings,
> It is an attribute to God himself;
> And earthly power doth then show likest God's
> When mercy seasons justice.
>
> (IV. i. 180–93)

Portia's lines shift the emphasis from the drama in the courtroom to the drama of salvation and damnation, alluding glancingly to the theological doctrine of Justification by Faith, while also echoing the injunction in the Apocrypha that 'Mercy is seasonable in the time of affliction, as clouds of rain in the time of drought' (Eccles. 35: 20). Earthly monarchs are presented not as exemplars of amoral power, defined by the 'dread and fear' they may inspire in their trembling subjects, but as praiseworthy and 'blest' when they recognize the limits of their power. Isabella in *Measure for Measure* makes use of similar analogies, in arguing against Angelo's rigid punitive conception of justice and the law, making a sharp distinction between 'proud man, | Dress'd in a little brief authority' (II. ii. 118–19) and a just and merciful God:

ISABELLA.   O, it is excellent
To have a giant's strength, but it is tyrannous
To use it like a giant . . .
Could great men thunder
As Jove himself does, Jove would ne'er be quiet,
For every pelting petty officer
Would use his heaven for thunder; nothing but thunder.

(*Measure for Measure*, II. ii. 108–14)

Though Portia addresses Shylock as a private individual, rather than as one exercising power in the state, the confrontation between Isabella and Angelo raises similar issues, in similar terms. Angelo speaks of the condemned Claudio as 'a forfeit of the law' and, like Shylock, sees the law as impersonal, to be obeyed literally: 'It is the law, not I, condemn your brother' (II. ii. 71, 80–1). Isabella responds with the same theological argument that Portia uses in addressing Shylock:

ISABELLA. Why, all the souls that were, were forfeit once,
And He that might the vantage best have took
Found out the remedy. How would you be
If He, which is the top of judgement, should
But judge you as you are? O, think on that,
And mercy then will breathe within your lips,
Like man new made.

(*Measure for Measure*, II. ii. 73–9)

All men are sinners: all, if judged on their merits alone, would deserve to be punished with the utmost severity. As Hamlet puts it, 'Use every man after his desert, and who shall scape whipping?' (*Hamlet*, II. ii. 524–5). Isabella, a postulant nun, makes this point in explicitly Christian terminology, referring to the 'remedy' of faith in Christ, as set forth in the gospels, where Portia, addressing Shylock as 'Jew', invokes the New Testament less overtly:

> Therefore Jew,
> Though justice be thy plea, consider this,
> That in the course of justice, none of us
> Should see salvation: we do pray for mercy,
> And that same prayer, doth teach us all to render
> The deeds of mercy.

(IV. i. 193–8)

In most productions I have seen, Shylock pauses for a moment at the end of Portia's speech, to build up suspense, but then he rejects her plea firmly, reasserting the position he has maintained throughout the trial scene. 'This strict court of Venice' (IV. i. 200) must pronounce sentence, without any mitigation or compassion for human fallibility: all men – Shylock himself as well as Antonio – must be answerable for their deeds.

> SHY. My deeds upon my head! I crave the law,
> The penalty and forfeit of my bond.

(IV. i. 202–3)

In an interesting essay, Hyam Maccoby argues a variant of the Danson–Coghill view of the play, restating the opposition between Old Testament and New Testament morality, the God of wrath and the God of love, in terms far more sympathetic to Shylock:

> The essence of the matter is that Shylock has a *Jewish point of view* – which, however, is represented by Shakespeare as theologically wrong, and as producing undesirable moral results in Shylock's character ... The accusation made through the character of Shylock is that the Jewish sense of justice ... is a moral and theological mistake, an expression of fundamental cruelty ... It is his refusal to abandon the Jewish standpoint which gives him grandeur. His faults are really Jewish virtues, as seen through Christian eyes. The faults of pride, obstinacy, heartlessness, and self-righteousness, translated into Jewish terms, become self-

85

respect, sense of justice and sense of responsibility. To understand the play, we have to understand how the Christian theology of Mercy translates the characteristic Jewish virtues into vices.[24]

This paradoxical reading, however partial, seems to me preferable to the reading of the play as Christian allegory, devoid of irony. To treat *The Merchant of Venice* as morality play, promulgating 'the Christian theology of Mercy', is to ignore the multiple ironies and shifting sympathies of the trial scene. When Coghill, for example, can blandly write off the humiliation and forced conversion of Shylock at the end of the scene as both just and merciful, in allowing Shylock 'his chance of eternal joy' where previously, as a Jew, he has been denied salvation, criticism approaches self-parody:

> It will, of course, be argued that it is painful for Shylock to swallow his pride, abjure his racial faith and receive baptism. But then Christianity is painful ... nor has it ever been held equally easy for all natures to embrace ... From Anthonio's point of view, Shylock has at least been given his chance of eternal joy, and it is he, Anthonio, that has given it to him.[25]

Other critics, more plausibly, have argued that the justice handed out to Shylock in the trial scene is injustice observing the outward forms of legality, an assertion of the hegemony of the Venetian Christian establishment, deploying the full power of the state to crush the interloper who dared to challenge it.[26]

In the course of the trial scene, Shylock is caught in a trap of his own making, as the disguised Portia, leading him on, demonstrates that a strict observance of the letter of the law not only invalidates the bond but threatens Shylock's life and livelihood.

> POR. For as thou urgest justice, be assur'd
> Thou shalt have justice more than thou desir'st.
>
> (IV. i. 311–12)

The reversal of fortune is underlined by having Gratiano taunt Shylock mercilessly, gloating over the Jew's discomfiture, with the same phrases Shylock himself had used in anticipating a verdict in his favour and a triumph over his enemies: 'an upright judge, a learned judge! ... a second Daniel, a Daniel, Jew!' (IV. i. 319, 329). It is hard not to feel a guilty complicity

here, rejoicing with Gratiano that Shylock has been thwarted
and Antonio saved: the delicate balance of sympathies in the
trial scene is illustrated by the choric use of the shallow,
vindictive Gratiano, representative of all that is worst in
Venetian society (Moody calls him a 'nether touchstone for
the Venetians'[27]). If the strict application of the law is cruel
as applied to Antonio, is it any less cruel, any more just, as
applied remorselessly to Shylock, vulnerable in his status as
alien? To both Gratiano and Shylock in this scene, law is
authorized violence.

Up to the point where Portia says 'Tarry a little', a moment
of maximum suspense in most productions, with Shylock's
knife approaching Antonio's bared breast, there is no reason to
expect any outcome of the trial other than the death of
Antonio, fulfilling the harsh and cruel letter of the law. A
formal verdict has been pronounced and Shylock holds his
knife in readiness:

> POR. A pound of that same merchant's flesh is thine,
>   The court awards it, and the law doth give it.
> SHY. Most rightful judge!
> POR. And you must cut this flesh from off his breast,
>   The law allows it, and the court awards it.
> *Shy.* Most learned judge! a sentence, come prepare.
>
> (IV. i. 295–300)

An earlier exchange between Shylock and the disguised Portia
foregrounds the possibility that Antonio might die onstage, as
Shylock, insisting on a strict construction of the language of the
bond, scornfully dismisses the appeal to 'charity' and civility:

> POR. Have by some surgeon Shylock on your charge,
>   To stop his wounds, lest he do bleed to death.
> SHY. Is it so nominated in the bond?
> POR. It is not so express'd, but what of that?
>   'Twere good you do so much for charity.
> SHY. I cannot find it, 'tis not in the bond.
>
> (IV. i. 253–8)

Using the weapons Shylock has handed her, Portia, in a
dazzling display of legal pyrotechnics, deploys 'an even more
literal and hypertechnical interpretation'[28] of the wording of

the bond, arguing first that the bond allows 'no jot of blood' but only and 'expressly' a pound of flesh (IV. i. 302–3), and, second, that since the bond stipulates 'a just pound' (IV. i. 323) and no more, if the amount of flesh cut off varies even slightly from that exact weight, he is subject to severe punishment under the laws of Venice.

> But in the cutting of it, if thou dost shed
> One drop of Christian blood, thy lands and goods
> Are (by the laws of Venice) confiscate
> Unto the state of Venice.

(IV. i. 305–8)

It has been argued that Portia's victory over Shylock is gained by a mere 'quibble', a trick, by which he is 'cheated out of his rights': once Shylock's bond is agreed to be valid, then the right to cut a pound of flesh would necessarily entail the shedding of blood.[29] But the dramatic effect of the scene, with its rapidfire series of reversals, is to turn the full force of the law on Shylock. As Moody says, the effect of Portia's 'legal cunning' is to put Shylock 'at the mercy of his enemies',[30] who can pretend to be generous while treating him with great severity, seizing his possessions and threatening his life.

> SHY. Shall I not have barely my principal?
> POR. Thou shalt have nothing but the forfeiture
> To be so taken at thy peril Jew.

(IV. i. 338–40)

With a repetition of 'Tarry' (we're not done with you yet), Portia has a further surprise for Shylock and the audience, invoking a law not previously mentioned by which Shylock's life and goods become forfeit.

> Tarry Jew,
> The law hath yet another hold on you.
> It is enacted in the laws of Venice,
> If it be proved against an alien,
> That by direct, or indirect attempts
> He seek the life of any citizen,
> The party 'gainst the which he doth contrive,
> Shall seize one half his goods, the other half
> Comes to the privy coffer of the state,

> And the offender's life lies in the mercy
> Of the Duke only . . .
>
> .   .   .   .   .   .
>
> Down therefore, and beg mercy of the Duke.
>
> (IV. i. 342–52, 359)

This law, applicable only to aliens and not to Venetian citizens, is, as Kornstein and others have argued, manifestly unfair and discriminatory, in its 'denial of equal protection of the laws' to Jews and other aliens.[31] What Shylock is taught in the latter part of the trial scene is that 'once again he is an outsider, without rights and utterly vulnerable'.[32] It is possible to interpret the actions of the Duke and Antonio when they have Shylock within their power as exemplifying the 'deeds of mercy' (IV. i. 198) that Portia recommended earlier in the scene. Yet their treatment of 'the offender' is harsh and punitive, a strict rendering-up of accounts, designed to humiliate Shylock and render him powerless. Shylock certainly does not see the confiscation of all his worldly goods, with half his possessions handed over to his enemy Antonio and a hint that 'humbleness' (IV. i. 368) on his part might eventually allow some of the rest to be returned to him, as an act of mercy.

> Nay, take my life and all, pardon not that –
> You take my house, when you do take the prop
> That doth sustain my house: you take my life
> When you do take the means whereby I live.
>
> (IV. i. 370–3)

Of the conditions imposed by Antonio and the Duke, the one that creates a particular feeling of unease in modern audiences is Shylock's forced conversion to Christianity. He is allowed no choice in the matter, since the Duke tells him that unless 'he presently become a Christian' (IV. i. 383) and agrees to make Lorenzo and Jessica his heirs, he will be put to death. Shakespeare gives Shylock very little to say at this point in the action: the words 'I am content' (IV. i. 389) are spoken by someone who cannot possibly be content, but has run out of ways of defending himself. His final words before he disappears from the play, scornfully dismissed by the victorious Christians, are those of a man who is utterly crushed:

89

> I pray you give me leave to go from hence,
> I am not well, – send the deed after me,
> And I will sign it.

$$(\text{IV. i. } 391\text{–}3)$$

As Brown has suggested, Shylock's virtual silence provides the 'means by which Shakespeare has drawn almost all the audience's interest to him once more', dominating the scene in his defeat, followed by a 'slow, silent exit'.[33] Actors have always relished this moment, giving them a chance for extra-textual elaboration. Olivier's offstage howl after leaving the stage is celebrated: he saw it as 'something to remain ringing in the ears long after [he] was in the dressing room'.[34] The trial scene, culminating in the humbling of Shylock, is the part of the play that comes closest to tragedy, evoking the standard Aristotelian emotions of pity and fear. After the scapegoat has been cast out, the rest of the characters are 'at liberty to enjoy the delights of Belmont'[35] and go about their everyday comic business.

5

Discord and Harmony

The structural problem of Act V is that it can seem anticlimactic, after the intense excitement of the trial scene. The play's most interesting character, the star audiences have paid their money to see, has departed the scene. A nineteenth-century German critic, quoted in the Variorum, finds the generic instability of the play, with its marked contrast in mood between Acts IV and V, a serious weakness:

> As soon as Shylock's fate is sealed in the Fourth Act, the public usually begins to arise and prepares to leave. To it Shylock's case is the main interest of the play . . . The discord between the tone of the comedy and the tragic tone of Shylock's fate cannot be denied. It cannot be denied that the deadly agony of that part of the play is not in accord with a Comedy; or that the Trial Scene, with its question of life or death, makes a far deeper impression than all the rest; and that a whole Act following thereon is, to the audience, intrusive and superfluous . . . No one denies that this last Act, with its beautiful language, is valuable; but with all its value as a final Act, it is a fault in composition.[1]

Uncomfortable with the radical discrepancy in tone between Acts IV and V, Irving and other Victorian actor-managers cut Act V radically or left it out altogether. Critics and directors who see 'Shylock and Antonio as the real protagonists of the piece', like H. B. Charlton, tend to dismiss Act V as 'superficial matter after the trial scene', provided by the dramatist, rather half-heartedly, to restore the characters and audience to a 'pleasant disposition' at the end of the play, dispelling any anxieties left over from Act IV.[2]

A very different view of Act V, argued by Burckhardt and others, is that the play's three principal motifs, the bond, the caskets, and the ring, are interwoven in a complex structural unity: 'The Merchant is a play about circularity and circulation; it asks how the vicious circle of the bond's law can be transformed into the ring of love'.[3] In this interpretation, Act V represents not an awkward change in mood, but the completion of a pattern. Danson and Barber see Act V as redemptive and life enhancing, placing particular emphasis on the recurrent imagery of music (a harmony that the disruptive Shylock 'would like to silence') and interpreting 'the test of the rings' as affirming 'the circle of charity, and the harmony of wedded love': 'No other comedy, until the late romances, ends with so full an expression of harmony as that which we get in the opening of the final scene of The Merchant of Venice. And no other final scene is so completely without irony about the joys it celebrates.'[4] In contrast, Moody finds a great deal of irony, along with 'harshness and dissonance', in the comic misunderstandings of Act V, and there is a similar emphasis on discord rather than harmony in commentaries on Act V by Newman, Kahn, and Belsey. 'The allusion to an ideal harmony of love has a critical function, and is not laid as a tribute before the Christians. Its effect is not to praise but to place them, to show how far from the ideal they are.'[5]

Act V of The Merchant of Venice is bathed in moonlight. One reason why Act V has given rise to such critical disagreement, as well as posing difficult problems for actors and directors, is that some of its most memorable passages have little apparent connection with the play's action. Lorenzo's disquisition on the music of the spheres is prefaced by instructions to musicians (to provide 'some welcome for the mistress of the house' (V. i. 38) when Portia returns), and is immediately followed by a stage direction indicating that the musicians, onstage, begin to play. But, though the dramatic context provides an occasion, it cannot account for the substance of the lines or make the lines particularly appropriate to Lorenzo, who speaks them:

> How sweet the moonlight sleeps upon this bank!
> Here we will sit, and let the sounds of music
> Creep in our ears – soft stillness and the night
> Become the touches of sweet harmony:
> Sit Jessica, – look how the floor of heaven
> Is thick inlaid with patens of bright gold,

There's not the smallest orb which thou behold'st
But in his motion like an angel sings,
Still quiring to the young-ey'd cherubins;
Such harmony is in immortal souls,
But whilst this muddy vesture of decay
Doth grossly close it in, we cannot hear it.

(v. i. 54–65)

The affective scene painting here, associating 'soft stillness and
the night' with music heard and unheard, is characteristic of
the first 100 lines or so of Act V, up to the entrance of the errant
husbands Bassanio and Gratiano (accompanied by the rather
different music of a trumpet call). Portia, on her entrance,
comments that things gain a good part of their meaning by
comparison, an awareness of difference and of proper 'season'
(v. i. 107):

POR. A substitute shines brightly as a king
    Until a king is by, and then his state
    Empties itself, as doth an inland brook
    Into the main of waters: music – hark!
NER. It is your music (madam) of the house.
POR. Nothing is good (I see), without respect, –
    Methinks it sounds much better than by day.

(v. i. 94–100)

In a sense, Lorenzo in the first part of the scene is acting as
Portia's 'substitute', with authority over Portia's household
until she and Bassanio return, and, in instructing Jessica (and
the audience) in what the eye of imagination is able to see and
the attentive ear can hear, he acts as her mentor, introducing
her to emotions and experiences that, behind the locked doors
of Shylock's house, she had not previously known. Jessica's
laconic response, 'I am never merry when I hear sweet music'
(v. i. 69), suggests some uncertainty or hesitation on her part.
In earlier scenes, one of them set at night, the lovers are
presented in much less exalted terms, as decidedly worldly in
their concerns.

JES. Here catch this casket, it is worth the pains.
    I am glad 'tis night – you do not look on me, –
    For I am much asham'd of my exchange:

> But love is blind, and lovers cannot see
> The pretty follies that themselves commit.
>
> (II. vi. 33–7)

One element of comparative 'respect' brought out explicitly in Lorenzo's speech in praise of 'the sweet power of music' is its evocation of a darker world from which the lovers have fled. Shylock is not named in the speech, but its details call him up, with his distrust of festivity, 'the vile squealing of the wry-neck'd fife' (II. v. 30), and his relentless pursuit of revenge against his enemies. The lines can be read as an attempt at exorcism, a casting out of the threatening stranger:

> The man that hath no music in himself,
> Nor is not moved with concord of sweet sounds,
> Is fit for treasons, stratagems, and spoils,
> The motions of his spirit are dull as night,
> And his affections dark as Erebus:
> Let no such man be trusted: – mark the music.
>
> (v. i. 83–8)

The note of distrust sounded here is present throughout Act V, complicating the moonlit lyricism of Belmont even in the love duet that begins the act.

It is possible to interpret the exchange between Lorenzo and Jessica at the beginning of Act V, evoking a hushed night-time scene, as an interlude of 'exquisite outdoor poetry',[6] reflecting a world of unalloyed love, without cares. Several productions I have seen, aided by a bright yellow moon and atmospheric lighting, have sought to bring out the romantic mood (compromised somewhat, in one case, by an inability of the production's Lorenzo and Jessica to speak the lines effectively). But the catalogue of loving couples, when closely examined, is disconcerting.

> LOR. The moon shines bright. In such a night as this,
>   When the sweet wind did gently kiss the trees,
>   And they did make no noise, in such a night
>   Troilus methinks mounted the Trojan walls,
>   And sigh'd his soul toward the Grecian tents
>   Where Cressid lay that night.
> JES.   In such a night
>   Did Thisbe fearfully o'ertrip the dew

> And saw the lion's shadow ere himself,
> And ran dismayed away.
> LOR.   In such a night
> Stood Dido with a willow in her hand
> Upon the wild sea banks, and waft her love
> To come again to Carthage.
> JES.   In such a night
> Medea gathered the enchanted herbs
> That did renew old Æson.

(v. i. 1–14)

The lovelorn Troilus, soon to be betrayed by Cressida; the fearful Thisbe, one of a doomed pair of lovers; the murderous sorceress Medea; and Dido, deserted by Aeneas: such figures are hardly role models for newlyweds. These familiar exempla, derived from Ovid and Chaucer (both of whom associate these unfortunate lovers with moonlight), set an ominous precedent for Lorenzo and Jessica, who, like them, profess a love in defiance of conventional familial and national boundaries.

As the exchange continues, Lorenzo makes the parallel overt, and Jessica, in response, casts herself as potential victim and Lorenzo in the role of the faithless, dissembling Jason or Aeneas.

> LOR.   In such a night
> Did Jessica steal from the wealthy Jew,
> And with an unthrift love did run from Venice,
> As far as Belmont.
> JES.   In such a night
> Did young Lorenzo swear he loved her well,
> Stealing her soul with many vows of faith,
> And ne'er a true one.
> LOR.   In such a night
> Did pretty Jessica (like a little shrew)
> Slander her love, and he forgave it her.

(v. i. 14–22)

There is of course an element of teasing here, with the lovers playing a game in which each tries to 'out-night' the other (v. i. 23), in verbal sparring where both the occasion and the subtext are erotic. Gilbert describes the passage as a kind of foreplay,[7], pointing out that many productions end the exchange with onstage caresses, hinting at offstage sexual pleasures in store. But Lorenzo's last speech here looks very much like an attempt to restore equilibrium, keeping the destructive forces at bay.

The main action of Act V is a continuation of the comic coda to Act IV, in which the disguised Portia attempts to trick the embarrassed Bassanio, indebted to her for saving Antonio's life, into surrendering his ring in violation of his pledge of fidelity. The Duke, Antonio, and Bassanio himself all make explicit that they consider themselves 'bound' to the supposed Balthazar, doctor of laws, by ties of courtesy, the expected way a gentleman should behave: 'you are much bound to him', 'We freely cope your courteous pains', 'And stand indebted over and above | In love and service to you evermore' (IV. i. 403, 408, 409–10). The 'doctor', playing the game by the rules, refuses compensation as indicative of a 'mercenary' mind – 'He is well paid that is well satisfied' (IV. i. 411, 414) – but, when pressed by Bassanio to take a token gift in 'remembrance' (IV. i. 418), Portia confronts him with an awkward choice, setting him a further test complementary to the earlier riddle of the caskets.

> POR. You press me far, and therefore I will yield,
>
> . . . . . .
>
> And (for your love) I'll take this ring from you, –
> Do not draw back your hand, I'll take no more,
> And you in love shall not deny me this!
> BASS. This ring good sir? alas it is a trifle,
> I will not shame myself to give you this!
> POR. I will have nothing else but only this,
> And now methinks I have a mind to it!
> BAS. There's more depends on this than on the value, –
> The dearest ring in Venice will I give you,
> And find it out by proclamation,
> Only for this I pray you pardon me!
> POR. I see sir you are liberal in offers, –
> You taught me first to beg, and now methinks
> You teach me how a beggar should be answer'd.
>
> (IV. i. 421–36)

Though the comic tone here differs markedly from the high drama shortly before, the emphasis on bonds and the problems they create provides a thematic unity. As Burckhardt points

96

out, 'the cost of redeeeming the public bond has been the forfeiture of the private one, the pledge of love'.[8] The conflict Bassanio faces here and later, when Portia upbraids him with his 'false heart' (v. i. 189) in breaking his promise, is between the marriage bond, given visible embodiment in the ring, and the invisible homosocial bonds of obligation and friendship. Playing her male role skilfully, the disguised Portia first tries to awaken Bassanio's sense of shame – he was 'beset with shame and courtesy', fearing a stain on his 'honour' for 'ingratitude', he claims later, in trying to apologize (v. i. 217–18) – and then denigrates the promises given to mere women. But it is Antonio's intervention, explicitly couched in terms of comparative value and the need to choose, that tips the balance:

> BASS. Good sir, this ring was given me by my wife,
>   And when she put it on, she made me vow
>   That I should neither sell, nor give, not lose it.
> POR. That scuse serves many men to save their gifts, –
>   And if your wife be not a mad-woman,
>   And know how well I have deserv'd this ring,
>   She would not hold out enemy for ever
>   For giving it to me: well, peace be with you!
>   *Exeunt [Portia and Nerissa]*
> ANT. My Lord Bassanio, let him have the ring,
>   Let his deservings and my love withal
>   Be valued 'gainst your wife's commandment.
>
>   (IV. i. 437–47)

As several critics have pointed out, a rivalry between Portia and Antonio is established here, to be developed more fully in Act V.[9] Which of us, Antonio is asking, do you love more? Which should take precedence, the love of friends, with its network of obligations, or the love of man and wife?

Antonio has only a few lines to speak in Act V, but his presence, as uncomfortable witness to the quarrel between Portia and Bassanio, is significant. The initial exchange between the reunited lovers features a series of puns by Portia on 'light' (the light of a candle and irresponsible, unfaithful wives) and 'bound' (bound in friendship, bound in contractual terms as surety for a debt, and also, perhaps, constrained or

disadvantaged), and ends with a rather unenthusiastic welcome, 'scant' in 'courtesy' (V. i. 141), extended to Antonio.

> POR. Let me give light, but let me not be light,
>   For a light wife doth make a heavy husband,
>   And never be Bassanio so for me, –
>   But God sort all: you are welcome home my lord.
> BASS. I thank you madam, – give welcome to my friend, –
>   This is the man, this is Antonio,
>   To whom I am so infinitely bound.
> POR. You should in all sense be much bound to him,
>   For (as I hear) he was much bound for you.
>
> (v. i. 129–37)

These somewhat barbed compliments are interrupted by
angry words from Gratiano and Nerissa, raising the issue of
marital infidelity in comic terms, insistently reductive in their
physicality, with Gratiano not so much justifying his action in
giving up Nerissa's ring as denigrating the ring itself as trivial
and contemptible. 'Would he were gelt', with its indecorous
threat of sexual violence, anticipates the theme of androgyny
and instability of gender, prominent later in the scene.

> GRA [to Nerissa]. By yonder moon I swear you do me wrong,
>   In faith I gave it to the judge's clerk, –
>   Would he were gelt that had it for my part,
>   Since you do take it (love) so much to heart.
> POR. A quarrel, ho, already! what's the matter?
> GRA. About a hoop of gold, a paltry ring
>   That she did give me, whose posy was
>   For all the world like cutler's poetry
>   Upon a knife, 'Love me, and leave me not'.
>
> (v. i. 142–50)

Nerissa's response, like Portia's a moment later, places the
ring's value not in its purchase price but in its symbolic
significance as token of the mutual obligations of man and
wife. Oaths are to be taken seriously, and not casually
dispensed with, in the pursuit of casual, transient pleasures.

> NER. What talk you of the posy or the value?
>   You swore to me when I did give it you,
>   That you would wear it till your hour of death,

And that it should lie with you in your grave, –
Though not for me, yet for your vehement oaths,
You should have been respective and have kept it.

(v. i. 151–6)

The conditions of the bestowal of the ring, of course, are
exactly those in the marriage ceremony of Bassanio and Portia.
What is ultimately at issue here, as all four squabbling lovers
recognize, is the fear of cuckoldry: that women, impatient with
a double standard that allows men a sexual freedom denied to
them, will retaliate by choosing new sexual partners just as
freely. Though Portia cautions Gratiano 'Speak not so grossly'
when he indignantly asks, 'What, are we cuckolds ere we have
deserv'd it?' (v. i. 265–6), the two women throughout the
homecoming scene consciously play on these potentially un-
manning fears, putting their husbands on the defensive.

As Belsey points out, in Act V Portia and Nerissa are setting
a riddle for their husbands and the audience. Unlike the riddle
of the caskets, here the two women know the answer, as does
the audience, while the husbands flounder in confusion,
unaware of the elegant solution.

> NER. Gave it a judge's clerk! no – God's my judge –
>   The clerk will ne'er wear hair on's face that had it.
> GRA. He will, and if he live to be a man.
> NER. Ay, if a woman live to be a man.
> GRA. Now (by this hand) I gave it to a youth,
>   A kind of boy, a little scrubbed boy,
>   No higher than thyself, the judge's clerk,
>   A prating boy that begg'd it as a fee.

(v. i. 157–64)

Paradoxically, 'all these utterances are true', however incompatible they appear to be, since 'the youth and the woman are
the same person',[10] as are the 'doctor' – 'no woman', according
to Bassanio – and 'some woman' who inveigled the ring from
Portia's inconstant spouse (v. i. 208–10). The answer to the
riddle lies in the androgyny of the Shakespearean comic
heroine (Gratiano's description, like Malvolio's description of
Cesario/Viola, quoted earlier, fits the boy actor playing the
role), and, more specifically, the cross-dressing that allows
Portia and Nerissa to have a double identity, unknown to their

99

husbands. Portia embarrasses Bassanio by pretending to praise him for unshaken constancy, and Bassanio's comic aside confirms the ascendancy she has established over him. In 'I dare be sworn for him' and the reference to worldly riches, there are echoes of two other ordeals or tests, Antonio's deadly bond and the riddle of the caskets.

> POR. I gave my love a ring, and made him swear
>   Never to part with it, and here he stands:
>   I dare be sworn for him he would not leave it,
>   Nor pluck it from his finger, for the wealth
>   That the world musters . . .
>   .   .   .   .   .   .
>
> BASS [Aside]. Why I were best to cut my left hand off,
>   And swear I lost the ring defending it.
>
>   (v. i. 170–4, 177–8)

When Bassanio confesses that he has given away the ring, marital amity is dissolved: rather than journeys that 'end in lovers meeting' (*Twelfth Night*, II. iii. 44), here the women threaten sexual rebellion on their first night together. The traditional happy ending of comedy is, for the moment at least, forestalled, seemingly subverted, as the women threaten to withhold their sexual favours, disavowing the marriage bond, as a token of their disapproval:

> POR. Even so void is your false heart of truth.
>   By heaven I will ne'er come in your bed
>   Until I see the ring!
> NER.   Nor I in yours
>   Until I again see mine!
>
>   (v. i. 189–92)

Like Jessica's ring, thoughtlessly traded away for a monkey, the circulating rings in *The Merchant of Venice* have several meanings: as well as being a visual symbol of marriage (as it still is in the wedding ceremony), the ring in Act V has a specifically sexual meaning, brought out in Gratiano's bawdy pun at the end of the play. Here 'Nerissa's ring' is equated with her genitals, which, he says, he will devote his attention to 'keeping safe' in his exclusive possession, guarding this 'ring' against potential sexual rivals (v. i. 306–7).[11] The wives, like the Athenian women in *Lysistrata*, are using a sexual weapon to keep their husbands in line. The threatened disruption is comic in tone, and the decorum of comedy governing Act V dictates an eventual peaceful resolution of the conflict, as does the controlling irony in Portia's knowledge, shared by the audience, that she can provide a solution for the riddles and act as agent of concord. But, at this moment, the discord is real, and the two husbands experience great difficulty in finding excuses for their behaviour.

The exchange between Bassanio and Portia has a ritualized formal patterning characteristic of Shakespearean comedy: we find something similar in *As You Like It*.

> SILVIUS. And so am I for Phebe.
> PHEBE. And I for Ganymede.
> ORLANDO. And I for Rosalind.
> ROSALIND. And I for no woman.
>
> *(As You Like It, v. ii. 84–7)*

Bassanio and Portia, like the mismatched lovers in *As You Like It*, are dancing to the same tune, playing out a pre-scripted courtship ritual. Yet though the controlling comic pattern is reflected in the insistent verse form, with its metrical balance and parallelism, there is no doubt that Portia wins the debate, maintains her dominant position, holding an advantage (like Rosalind) by virtue of her superior knowledge, shared by the audience. Any final resolution of the conflict, it is implied, will be on her terms and not his.

> BASS.   Sweet Portia,
> If you did know to whom I gave the ring,
> If you did know for whom I gave the ring,
> And would conceive for what I gave the ring,
> And how unwillingly I left the ring,
> When nought would be accepted but the ring,
> You would abate the strength of your displeasure.
> POR. If you did known the virtue of the ring,
> Or half her worthiness that gave the ring,
> Or your own honour to contain the ring,
> You would not then have parted with the ring.
>
> (v. i. 192–202)

101

Though Bassanio feebly seeks to defend himself, claiming that his 'honour' would not allow him to incur the reputation of 'ingratitude' towards someone instrumental in saving the life of his 'dear friend' (v. i. 214–19), Portia presses home her advantage, reminding him of her own power to hurt. Construing his betrayal as sexual, she announces that she will retaliate in kind: since he has given away his 'jewel', she will feel free to bestow hers wherever she pleases. This direct sexual threat warns her husband how easily marital peace can turn into warfare: 'Cuckoo, cuckoo! O, word of fear | Unpleasing to a married ear!' (*Love's Labour's Lost*, v. ii. 889–90). She is an independent agent and, she reminds him, he cannot take her fidelity or obedience for granted.

> POR. Let not that doctor e'er come near my house –
> Since he hath got the jewel that I loved,
> And that which you did swear to keep for me,
> I will become as liberal as you,
> I'll not deny him anything I have,
> No, not my body, nor my husband's bed:
> Know him I shall, I am well sure of it.
> Lie not a night from home. Watch me like Argus, –
> If you do not, if I be left alone,
> Now by mine honour (which is yet mine own)
> I'll have that doctor for my bedfellow.
> NER. And I his clerk: therefore be well advis'd
> How you do leave me to mine own protection.
>
> (v. i. 223–35)

The disruptive, unsettling challenge to patriarchal assumptions here is very different from Portia's demure submission to the conquering hero after he has solved the riddle of the caskets, presenting herself as a 'gentle spirit' content 'to be directed' in all things by her husband 'As from her lord, her governor, her king' (III. ii. 163–5). Portia in Act V deliberately unleashes fears of emasculating humiliation similar to those exploited by Iago ('Look to your wife' (III. iii. 200)) to undermine Othello's confident façade:

> OTH.   O curse of marriage
> That we can call these delicate creatures ours
> And not their appetites!
>
> (*Othello*, III. iii. 272–4)

Given the chance, both passages imply, all women will turn whore. Portia's motive, of course, is quite unlike Iago's, and she wishes ultimately to restore or redefine equilibrium, not destroy it. As Kahn says, Portia and Nerissa are teaching their errant husbands 'a lesson about the primacy of their marital obligations over their obligations to their male friends', warning them that, if they default on these responsibilities, their wives will seek revenge by betraying them.[12]

Antonio, a silent presence throughout the scene, then accurately observes, 'I am th'unhappy subject of these quarrels' (v. i. 238). Several recent productions in their staging have placed Antonio centre stage between Portia and Bassanio, 'emphasizing that the quarrel is not just about the rings but about Antonio and his relationship to Bassanio'.[13] After Bassanio, begging pardon, swears never again to 'break an oath' sworn to Portia, Antonio intervenes, offering to act as 'surety' a second time for Bassanio (v. i. 248, 254), in a speech that consciously recalls his earlier bond with Shylock as guarantor for Bassanio's debt.

> I once did lend my body for his wealth,
> Which but for him that had your husband's ring
> Had quite miscarried. I dare be bound again,
> My soul upon the forfeit, that your lord
> Will never more break faith advisedly.
>
> (v. i. 249–53)

'Lend my body' suggests a kind of marriage ceremony, signifying a willingness to die for his beloved friend, and 'my soul upon the forfeit' makes the stakes even higher, in saying that this time Antonio will wager his immortal soul, risking his chance of salvation. Though the lines take the form of a pledge (with a 'forfeit' attached), they are a symbolic sundering of bonds, acknowledging the primacy of Portia's claim as wife, by which he 'relinquishes any hold on' Bassanio.[14] In production, this has become 'the moment in which Antonio promises never to interfere again',[15] and nearly all productions I have seen have emphasized Antonio's loneliness in the closing moments of Act V, odd man out among all the couples.

Antonio's attempt to act as peacemaker, mediating the dispute between husband and wife, is ineffectual, and indeed makes matters worse. When Portia hands him a ring to give to Bassanio, then the horrified Bassanio recognizes the ring he had already lost to the 'doctor' in Venice. The threat of adultery, nightmarishly, has metamorphosed into seeming reality, with 'pardon me', as against its normal meaning, becoming the wives' cry of triumph over their husbands.

> POR. Then you shall be his surety: give him this,
>   And bid him keep it better than the other.
> ANT. Here lord Bassanio, swear to keep this ring.
> BASS. By heaven it is the same I gave the doctor!
> POR. I had it of him: pardon me Bassanio,
>   For by this ring the doctor lay with me.
> NER. And pardon me my gentle Gratiano,
>   For that same scrubbed boy (the doctor's clerk)
>   In lieu of this, last night did lie with me.
>
> (v. i. 254–62)

The men are 'all amaz'd' and baffled, reduced to an impotence that is only reinforced ('I am dumb!', Antonio exclaims) when Portia reveals the answer to the riddle (v. i. 266, 279). Revelling in her power, which she can now portray as benevolent, Portia lets them in on the secret of her double identity, male and female, thus clearing herself of any charge of adultery. Bassanio's expression of gratitude and relief recognizes that Portia is in effect two people – as it were, a female warrior, able to play an active or a passive role:

> BASS. Sweet doctor, you shall be my bedfellow, –
>   When I am absent then lie with my wife.
>
> (v. i. 284–5)

Her power seems limitless, as she scatters her largesse to all around her. To Antonio, she provides far 'better news' than he expects, in the magical restoration of his wealth, once thought irretrievably lost, and to Lorenzo and Jessica she brings a deed of gift, drawn up at the end of Act IV, making them heirs to 'the rich Jew' – 'manna', Lorenzo says, for 'starved people' (v. i. 274, 291–5).

One way in which Acts IV and V are linked, though in tone and dramatic pattern one approaches tragedy and the other is predominantly comic, is that each can be seen as embodying

Portia's triumph. In the trial scene, given a chance in her male dress to display hitherto unsuspected powers, she defeats a formidable adversary by her forensic skills and her knowledge, cannily withheld until the moment of greatest dramatic tension, of exactly those Venetian laws that will save Antonio and condemn Shylock. By implication, Portia in Act IV ('so young a body with so old a head') refutes those assumptions of a patriarchal society that relegate women to a position of ignorant subordination – assumptions she herself had endorsed earlier in calling herself 'an unlesson'd girl, unschool'd, unpractised', eager for tuition by her husband (IV. i. 160–1; III. ii. 159). In Act V, it is again knowledge withheld that constitutes a primary source of her power, though her social status, with the confidence gained from managing a great estate, contributes to her ability to direct and control the action. Here it is the fallible husbands, initially content in the 'ordinary condition of moral compromise' and 'cosy amorality' characteristic of Venetian society,[16] who are given necessary tuition, educated in a reality more complex and problematical than they had assumed it to be.

The Merchant of Venice, throughout its long production history, has shown a similar capacity for surprising and challenging its audience. It is the way it keeps asking difficult questions, undermining the received ideas of characters and audience – about Jews and Christians, about women, about generosity, about friendship, enmity, and the construction of the Other, about justice and the law – that makes *The Merchant of Venice* such a great play, and such an unsettling one.

Notes

INTRODUCTION

1. Quoted in John Wilders (ed.), *Shakespeare, The Merchant of Venice: A Casebook* (London: Macmillan, 1969), 25.
2. Northrop Frye, *An Anatomy of Criticism* (Princeton: Princeton University Press, 1957), 165.
3. Derek Cohen, 'Shakespeare and the Idea of the Jew', in *Shakespearean Motives* (London: Macmillan, 1988), 104.
4. Arnold Wesker, *Shylock and Other Plays* (London: Penguin, 1990), 177–9.
5. Michiko Katukani, 'Debate over Shylock Simmers once again', *New York Times*, 22 Feb. 1981, section 2, p. 30.
6. James Shapiro, *Shakespeare and the Jews* (New York: Columbia University Press, 1996), 89–117.
7. E. E. Stoll, *Shakespeare Studies* (New York: Macmillan, 1927), 280.
8. Ibid. 269, 273; for a contrary view, see Charles Edelman, 'Which is the Jew that Shakespeare Knew?: Shylock on the Elizabethan Stage', *Shakespeare Survey*, 52 (1999), 99–106.
9. Shapiro, *Shakespeare and the Jews*, 1.
10. John Russell Brown, 'The Realization of Shylock: A Theatrical Criticism', in John Russell Brown and Bernard Harris (eds.), *Early Shakespeare* (Stratford-upon Avon Studies; London: Edward Arnold, 1961), 193.
11. Quoted in *The Merchant of Venice*, ed. W. W. Furness (New Variorum Edition; Philadelphia: J. B. Lippincott Company, 1916), 427.
12. Quoted in ibid. 450–1.
13. Quoted in ibid. 452.
14. Quoted in Brown, 'The Realization of Shylock', 194.
15. There is some uncertainty as to how often Irving performed a version of the play omitting Act V. According to Alan Hughes (*Henry Irving, Shakespearean* (Cambridge: Cambridge University Press, 1981), 227), the play was 'usually presented intact', except for several performances in 1880, but both Bulman and Lelyveld say that both versions were performed between 1880 and 1905: 'he was able to do with or without the fifth act, as mood or policy prompted him' (Toby Lelyveld, *Shylock on the*

Stage (London: Routledge & Kegan Paul, 1961), 93). Even when Irving did perform Act V, it was heavily cut.

16. Northrop Frye, 'The Argument of Comedy', in *English Institute Essays, 1948* (New York: Columbia University Press, 1949). 68–73.

17. Lawrence Danson, *The Harmonies of* The Merchant of Venice (New Haven: Yale University Press, 1978), 13, 61.

18. Ibid. 50, 52, 57. For similar arguments, see Neville Coghill, 'The Basis of Shakespearian Comedy' (1950), in *Collected Papers* (Brighton: Harvester, 1998); and Barbara Lewalski, 'Biblical Allusion and Allegory in *The Merchant of Venice*', *Shakespeare Quarterly*, 13 (1962), 321–43.

19. A. D. Moody, *Shakespeare: The Merchant of Venice* (London: Edward Arnold, 1964), 10, 31.

20. Ibid. 16-17.

21. Karen Newman, 'Portia's Ring: Unruly Women and Structures of Exchange in *The Merchant of Venice*', *Shakespeare Quarterly*, 38 (1987), 19.

22. Ibid. 23.

23. Walter Cohen, '*The Merchant of Venice* and the Possibilities of Historical Criticism', *ELH* 49 (1982), 767, 771, 773.

24. Jonathan Miller, *Subsequent Performances* (London: Faber & Faber, 1986), 155.

25. Bill Overton, *The Merchant of Venice: Text and Performance* (Basingstoke: Macmillan, 1987), 45; James C. Bulman, *Shakespeare in Performance: The Merchant of Venice* (Manchester: Manchester University Press, 1991), 83.

26. Quoted in *The Merchant of Venice*, ed. Furness, 435.

27. Bulman, *Shakespeare in Performance*, 40.

CHAPTER 1. STRANGERS AND VENETIANS

1. Jean-Paul Sartre, *Anti-Semite and Jew*, trans. George J. Becker (New York: Schocken Books, 1948), 69.

2. James Shapiro, *Shakespeare and the Jews* (New York: Columbia University Press, 1996), 72–6.

3. Brian Pullan, *The Jews of Europe and the Inquisition of Venice, 1550–1670* (Oxford: Blackwell, 1983), 146.

4. Brian Pullan, *Rich and Poor in Renaissance Venice* (Oxford: Blackwell, 1971), 442.

5. David Chambers and Brian Pullan (eds.), *Venice: A Documentary History, 1450–1630* (Oxford: Blackwell, 1993), 325.

6. John Gillies, *Shakespeare and the Geography of Difference* (Cambridge: Cambridge University Press, 1994),124.

7. Lewkenor's translation was published in 1599, and it is generally accepted that Shakespeare read it before writing *Othello*: see, e.g., the Arden edition of *Othello*, ed. E. A. J. Honigmann (1997), 5–8. The 1596–7 date of *The Merchant of Venice* would argue against Contarini as a direct source for details in that play. But Christopher Whitfield ('Sir Lewis Lewkenor and "The Merchant of Venice": A Suggested Connexion', *N&Q* 209 (1964), 123–39) has shown that Lewkenor's translation was circulating in MS

before 1595, and that Shakespeare is very likely to have known Lewkenor at this time. It is thus possible that Lewkenor served as oral source (for the treatment of Venetian justice or Venetian wealth) or that Shakespeare had access to the manuscript.

8. Gaspare Contarini, *The Commonwealth and Government of Venice*, trans. Lewis Lewkenor (1599), facsimile reprint (Amsterdam: Da Capo Press, 1969), 1.

9. Shapiro, *Shakespeare and the Jews*, 183.

10. Contarini, *The Commonwealth and Government of Venice*, 139–40.

11. Quoted in Robert Finlay, *Politics in Renaissance Venice* (London: Ernest Benn, 1980), 33.

12. Contarini, *The Commonwealth and Government of Venice*, 40

13. Ibid. 41–2.

14. Ibid., sig. A3.

15. Zera S. Fink, *The Classical Republicans* (Evanston, Ill.: Northwestern University Press, 1945), 49, 126. There have been many recent studies of English republicanism in the seventeenth century, and of the influence of the Venetian model, as embodied in Contarini. See especially J. G. A. Pocock, *The Machiavellian Moment* (Princeton: Princeton University Press, 1975), David Norbrook, *Writing the English Republic* (Cambridge: Cambridge University Press, 1999), and, an earlier study that particularly emphasizes Contarini's influence on later writers, Z. S. Fink, *The Classical Republicans* (1945). Pocock says of Contarini: 'In his ideal constitution it is the laws that rule, and the distribution of authority between one, few, and many is a means of keeping all three subject to law and reason' (p. 325).

16. Pullan, *The Jews of Europe*, 153.

17. Shapiro, *Shakespeare and the Jews*, 182–3.

18. Ibid. 187.

19. Thomas Wilson, *A Discourse upon Usury* (1572), ed. R. H. Tawney (London: G. Bell & Sons, 1925), 229.

20. Ibid. 242, 249

21. Francis Bacon, *The Essays*, ed. John Pitcher (Harmondsworth: Penguin Books, 1985), 185.

22. Wilson, *A Discourse upon Usury*, 265.

23. Benjamin Nelson, *The Idea of Usury*, 2nd edn. (Chicago: University of Chicago Press, 1969), 75–9.

24. Wilson, *A Discourse upon Usury*, 63.

25. Bacon, *The Essays*, 184.

26. Quoted in W. H. Auden, *The Dyer's Hand and Other Essays* (New York: Vintage Books, 1968), 224.

27. John Russell Brown, *Shakespeare and his Comedies* (London: Methuen, 1962), 62.

28. Auden, *The Dyer's Hand*, 225.

29. Brown, *Shakespeare and his Comedies*, 67.

30. John W. Draper, 'Usury in *The Merchant of Venice*', *Modern Philology*, 33 (1935), 38.

31. Lars Engle, "'Thrift is Blessing'": Exchange and Explanation in *The Merchant of Venice'*, *Shakespeare Quarterly*, 37 (1986), 20; Leslie Fiedler, *The Stranger in Shakespeare* (New York: Stein & Day, 1972), 88.
32. For further discussion of these aspects of the trial scene, see Ch. 4.
33. Auden, *The Dyer's Hand*, 229.

CHAPTER 2. SOME VERSIONS OF SHYLOCK

1. E. E. Stoll, *Shakespeare Studies* (New York: Macmillan, 1927), 296–7; for Stoll, Shylock is as money-lender and Jew an object of 'popular detestation and ridicule', and Shakespeare's Shylock differs very little from his 'acknowledged prototype', Marlowe's Barrabas. See *The Merchant of Venice*, ed. Jay L. Halio (Oxford: Oxford University Press, 1993), 10–11, for a similar view that 'Shakespeare's initial conception of him was essentially as a comic villain' with grotesque wig and false nose. Edelman, in contrast, argues that 'there is no reliable contemporary evidence whatsoever' that would support 'the so-called Elizabethan stereotype of the villainous stage Jew' (Charles Edelman, 'Which is the Jew that Shakespeare Knew?: Shylock on the Elizabethan Stage', *Shakespeare Survey*, 52 (1999), 99). In 1898, William Poel presented a comic Shylock, complete with red wig, false nose, and 'a good deal of clowning', in what he claimed to be an 'authentic' production, for the Elizabethan Stage Society: see John Gross, *Shylock: Four Hundred Years in the Life of a Legend* (London: Vintage, 1994), 153–5.
2. Thomas W. Baldwin, *The Organization and Personnel of the Shakespearean Company* (Princeton: Princeton University Press, 1927),178–81, 231–5, 246–9.
3. [George Granville,] *The Jew of Venice. A Comedy* (London, 1701, sig. A4ᵛ, quoted from a facsimile reprint (London: Cornmarket Press, 1969). The play's closing lines, spoken by Bassanio, may indicate the tone of Granville's adaptation:
   Love, like a Meteor, shows a short-liv'd Blaze,
   Or treads thro' various Skies, a wond'ring Maze,
   Begot by Fancy, and by Fancy led,
   Here in a Moment, in a Moment fled:
   But fixt by Obligation, it will last;
   For Gratitude's the Charm that binds it fast.
4. Philip H. Highfill et al., *A Biographical Dictionary of Actors, Actresses . . . and Other Stage Personnel in London, 1660-1800*, 16 vols. (Carbondale and Edwardsville, Ill.: Southern Illinois University Press, 1973–93), iv. 444, 450.
5. Gross, *Shylock*, 92.
6. *The Merchant of Venice*, ed. Halio, 63.
7. John Russell Brown, 'The Realization of Shylock: A Theatrical Criticism', in John Russell Brown and Bernard Harris (eds.), *Early Shakespeare* (Stratford-upon Avon Studies; London: Edward Arnold, 1961), 188–9.
8. Gross, *Shylock*, 95.
9. Brown, 'The Realization of Shylock', 189.

10. Gross, *Shylock*, 110, 111, 113.
11. Brown, 'The Realization of Shylock', 193.
12. Quoted in *The Merchant of Venice*, ed. W. W. Furness (New Variorum Edition; Philadelphia: J. B. Lippincott Company, 1916), 427.
13. Toby Lelyveld, *Shylock on the Stage* (London: Routledge & Kegan Paul, 1961), 81.
14. Gross, *Shylock*, 128; James C. Bulman, *Shakespeare in Performance: The Merchant of Venice* (Manchester: Manchester University Press, 1991), 29, 32.
15. Lelyveld, *Shylock on the Stage*, 85.
16. Bernard Shaw, *Our Theatres in the Nineties*, 3 vols. (London: Constable, 1948), ii. 198.
17. Bulman, *Shakespeare in Performance*, 37–8; Ellen Terry, quoted in Hughes, 232.
18. Bulman, *Shakespeare in Performance*, 47.
19. Ibid. 49.
20. Brown, 'The Realization of Shylock', 195.
21. Shaw, *Our Theatres in the Nineties*, ii. 198.
22. Jonathan Miller, *Subsequent Performances* (London: Faber & Faber, 1986), 35, 105, 107.
23. Ibid. 159.
24. Ibid. 107.
25. Irving Wardle's review, headed 'Merchants All' (*The Times*, 20 Apr. 1970), emphasizes the way in which the Belmont scenes as well as the Venetian scenes in this production are 'a total departure from stage tradition', which 'unmasks the romantic element as so much flimsy sentimental decoration'. The review is reprinted in James C. Bulman and H. C. Coursen (eds.), *Shakespeare on Television* (Hanover, NH: University Press of New England, 1988), 244–5.
26. Bulman, *Shakespeare in Performance*, 93.
27. Miller, *Subsequent Performances*, 107.
28. Laurence Olivier, *On Acting* (London: Sceptre, 1987), 113.
29. Bulman, *Shakespeare in Performance*, 101.
30. Quoted in ibid. 107.
31. John Barton, *Playing Shakespeare* (London: Methuen, 1984), 174, 177.
32. Philip Brockbank, *Players of Shakespeare* (Cambridge: Cambridge University Press, 1985), 13; Barton, *Playing Shakespeare*, 170.
33. Ibid. 180.
34. Brockbank, *Players of Shakespeare*, 17–18; Barton, *Playing Shakespeare*, 172.
35. Brockbank, *Players of Shakespeare*, 15–17.
36. Barton, *Playing Shakespeare*, 172, 175.
37. Ibid. 171, 172.
38. Ibid. 171.
39. Ibid. 174.
40. Quoted in Judith Cook, *Shakespeare's Players* (London: Harrap, 1983), 82.
41. Brockbank, *Players of Shakespeare*, 21; Cook, *Shakespeare's Players*, 83.
42. Barton, *Playing Shakespeare*, 175.
43. Quoted in Brockbank, *Players of Shakespeare*, 22.
44. Barton, *Playing Shakespeare*, 176–9; Brockbank, *Players of Shakespeare*, 23.

45. Cook, *Shakespeare's Players*, 84–5.
46. Brockbank, *Players of Shakespeare*, 30, 39.
47. Barton, *Playing Shakespeare*, 179; Cook, *Shakespeare's Players*, 86.
48. Brockbank, *Players of Shakespeare*, 14; Ann Jennalie Cook, in *Shakespeare Quarterly*, 30 (1979), 160.
49. Bill Overton, *The Merchant of Venice: Text and Performance* (Basingstoke: Macmillan, 1987), 55, 62–3.
50. The one unequivocally favourable review was by Andrew Rissik, *Independent*, 1 May 1987. Michael Billington (*Guardian*, 1 May 1987) and John Peter (*Sunday Times*, 3 May 1987) had reservations about the production, but praise for Sher's performance. Negative reviews, which note the emphasis on the play's 'moral ugliness' in this production, included Mary Harron (*Observer*, 3 May 1987); Charles Osborne (*Daily Telegraph*, 1 May 1987); Charles Spencer (*Daily Telegraph*, 29 Apr. 1988); and Jeremy Kingston (*The Times*, 27 Apr. 1988).
51. *Sunday Times*, 3 May 1987; *The Times*, 27 April 1988.
52. Bulman, *Shakespeare in Performance*, 135; *Sunday Times*, 3 May 1987.
53. Bulman, *Shakespeare in Performance*, 119, 121.
54. Ibid. 120, 123.
55. Ibid. 119.
56. Ibid. 125–31.
57. *Shakespeare Survey*, 43 (1990), 188.
58. See the favourable reviews of this production by Lois Potter (*Shakespeare Quarterly*, 50 (1999), 74–6); and Richard Proudfoot (*Shakespeare Survey*, 52 (1999), 216–21). Proudfoot commented on how Magni, who 'had the audience eating out of his hand', serving as 'mediator between stage and auditorium', evoked the tradition of Will Kempe, in which the clown was 'the dominant figure in Elizabethan acting companies' (pp. 219–21). Not all the reviews were this positive: the *TLS* reviewer (12 Feb. 1999) thought the production trivialized the play, as did Nicholas de Jongh (*Evening Standard*, 1 June 1998).
59. Reviews of John Peter (*The Times*, 9 Jan. 2000); Robert Butler (*Independent on Sunday*, 19 Dec. 1999); interview with Trevor Nunn for television broadcast of the NT video (www.pbs.org/wgbh/masterpiece/merchant).
60. *Guardian*, 18 June 1999.
61. Ibid., 1 Feb. 2000.
62. Brockbank, *Players of Shakespeare*, 29, 37, 39.
63. Ibid. 39.
64. John Peter, *Sunday Times*, 27 June 1999.
65. Miller, *Subsequent Performances*, 35, 55, 96.
66. Bulman, *Shakespeare in Performance*, 57, 65, 72. According to Halio, a 1957 production at the Oregon Shakespeare Festival followed the example of William Poel in presenting an 'authentic' Elizabethan staging, with a comic Shylock in red wig and false nose (*The Merchant of Venice*, ed. Halio, 81).
67. Maria Verch, 'The Merchant of Venice on the German Stage since 1945', *Theatre History Studies*, 5 (1985), 85, 91; Gross, *Shylock*, 203–8.
68. Bulman, *Shakespeare in Performance*, 120–2.

69. Cook, *Shakespeare's Players*, 85.
70. Roger Savage, *TLS*, 8 September 1995.
71. Ruth Nevo, *Comic Transformations in Shakespeare* (London: Methuen, 1980), 130.

CHAPTER 3. 'O THAT I WERE A MAN!'

1. Lisa Jardine, *Still Harping on Daughters* (London: Harvester, 1989), 17, 29. Jardine argues that 'whenever Shakespeare's female characters in the comedies draw attention to their own androgyny ... the resulting eroticism is to be associated with their *maleness* rather than with their *femaleness*' (p. 20). Stephen Orgel, in *Impersonations*, also finds an erotic element in theatrical cross-dressing, but does not equate androgyny with homoerotic desire. With particular reference to *As You Like It*, he writes: 'eroticized boys appear to be a middle term between men and women, and far from precluding the love of women, they are represented as *enabling* figures, as a way of getting from men to women' (Stephen Orgel, *Impersonations* (Cambridge: Cambridge University Press, 1996), 63).
2. Ibid. 63; Catherine Belsey, 'Disrupting Sexual Difference: Meaning and Gender in the Comedies', in John Drakakis (ed.), *Alternative Shakespeares* (London: Routledge, 1988), 185–90. See also the careful and illuminating discussion of ways in which cross-dressing in *As You Like It*, *Twelfth Night*, and *The Merchant of Venice* 'reveals the constructed nature of patriarchy's representations of the feminine' in Jean E. Howard, 'Crossdressing, the Theatre, and Gender Struggle in Early Modern England', *Shakespeare Quarterly*, 39 (1988),. 430–5. Howard sees the three plays as differing in the extent to which their treatment of gender roles is conservative and 'recuperative' or is more 'subversive'.
3. Belsey, 'Disrupting Sexual Difference', 187.
4. Ibid. 180.
5. Clara Claiborne Park, 'As We Like It: How a Girl can be Smart and still Popular', in Carol Lenz, Gayle Greene, and Carol Neely (eds.), *The Woman's Part: Feminist Criticism of Shakespeare* (Urbana, Ill.: University of Illinois Press, 1983), 108, 111.
6. Howard, 'Crossdressing, the Theatre, and Gender Struggle', 434–5; Belsey, 'Disrupting Sexual Difference', 180.
7. Howard, 'Crossdressing, the Theatre, and Gender Struggle', 427. According to Howard, Portia's actions 'reveal that masculine prerogatives are based on custom, not nature, since a woman can indeed successfully assume masculine positions of authority', though 'the incipient subversiveness' of her initiatives in the latter half of the play is limited. 'Portia's actions are not aimed at letting her occupy a man's place indefinitely, but at making her own place in a patriarchy more bearable' (p. 433). Park argues a similar position: though her scope of action is restricted, nevertheless 'alone of Shakespeare's heroines, Portia is allowed to confront a man over matters outside a woman's sphere, and to win' ('As We Like It', 108). The 'containment' thesis, arguing that in Renaissance drama 'the

subversive voices are produced by and within the affirmations of order' and 'do not undermine that order', is powerfully argued by Stephen Greenblatt in 'Invisible Bullets' (Stephen Greenblatt, *Shakespearean Negotiations* (Oxford: Clarendon Press, 1988), 52).

8. Lisa Jardine, *Reading Shakespeare Historically* (London: Routledge, 1996), 58.
9. Leslie Fiedler, *The Stranger in Shakespeare* (New York: Stein & Day, 1972), 114; A. D. Moody, *Shakespeare: The Merchant of Venice* (London: Edward Arnold, 1964), 36. In Moody's reading, Portia gives only lip service to the terms of her father's will, 'observes the terms of the lottery while exerting as much influence on the result as she may' (p. 36). For an account of the treatment of this scene in Miller's 1970 production, see James C. Bulman, *Shakespeare in Performance: The Merchant of Venice* (Manchester: Manchester University Press, 1991), 87.
10. Lawrence Danson, *The Harmonies of* The Merchant of Venice (New Haven: Yale University Press, 1978), 117–18.
11. Philip Brockbank, *Players of Shakespeare* (Cambridge: Cambridge University Press, 1985), 33, 36.
12. W. H. Auden, *The Dyer's Hand and Other Essays* (New York: Vintage Books, 1968), 222.
13. Fiedler, *The Stranger in Shakespeare*, 101–6.
14. Catherine Belsey, 'Love in Venice', *Shakespeare Survey*, 44 (1991), 43.
15. Keith Geary, 'The Nature of Portia's Victory: Turning to Men in *The Merchant of Venice*', *Shakespeare Survey*, 37 (1984), 62.
16. John Russell Brown, *Shakespeare and his Comedies* (London: Methuen, 1962), 67; C. L. Barber, *Shakespeare's Festive Comedy* (Princeton: Princeton University Press, 1972), 171.
17. Walter Cohen, 'The *Merchant of Venice* and the Possibilities of Historical Criticism', *ELH* 49 (1982), 776.
18. Geary, 'The Nature of Portia's Victory', 62.
19. Brown, *Shakespeare and his Comedies*, 67.
20. Jardine, *Reading Shakespeare Historically*, 62.
21. Karen Newman, 'Portia's Ring: Unruly Women and Structures of Exchange in *The Merchant of Venice*', *Shakespeare Quarterly*, 38 (1987), 19–33.; cf. Park, 'As We Like It', 111.
22. Jardine, *Reading Shakespeare Historically*, 62–3.
23. Auden, *The Dyer's Hand*, 232.
24. Danson, *The Harmonies of* The Merchant of Venice, 49.
25. Auden, *The Dyer's Hand*, 231.
26. Graham Midgley, 'The *Merchant of Venice*: A Reconsideration', in John Wilders (ed.), *Shakespeare*, The Merchant of Venice: *A Casebook* (London: Macmillan, 1969), 199.
27. On the emphasis on overt homosexuality in recent productions, see my discussion of the 1987 production directed by Bill Alexander in Ch. 2, and cf. Bulman, *Shakespeare in Performance*, 125–30. Keith Geary has argued that 'such directorial touches both recognize an important element in the play and falsify the manner in which Shakespeare presents it' by overinsistence on 'intimate physical contact' ('The Nature of Portia's Victory', 60). In an interesting discussion, Fiedler has commented on similarities with another

Antonio, doting on the unresponsive Sebastian in *Twelfth Night* ('But come what may, I do adore thee so, That danger shall seem sport' (ii. i. 46–7)), and with the sonnets, especially sonnet 20 (*The Stranger in Shakespeare*, 89–95).

28. Coppélia Kahn, 'The Cuckoo's Note: Male Friendship and Cuckoldry in *The Merchant of Venice*', in Peter Erickson and Coppélia Kahn (eds.), *Shakespeare's 'Rough Magic'* (Newark, Del.: University of Delaware Press, 1985), 107.

CHAPTER 4. 'I STAND FOR JUDGMENT'

1. As Miriam Gilbert points out, every RSC production since 1956 has had an interval break after the scene between Shylock and Tubal (Act III, Scene i), ending with Shylock's vow of revenge, and at least two recent productions have included after Jessica's flight in Act II, Scene vi, a version of 'Shylock's return', a lone figure among a crowd of revellers: see Miriam Gilbert, *Shakespeare at Stratford: The Merchant of Venice* (London: Arden Shakespeare, 2002), 41–3, 111–15.

2. Sigurd Burckhardt, '*The Merchant of Venice*: The Gentle Bond', in John Wilders (ed.), *Shakespeare, The Merchant of Venice: A Casebook* (London: Macmillan, 1969), 218.

3. *The Merchant of Venice*, ed. A. Quiller-Couch and J. Dover Wilson (Cambridge: Cambridge University Press, 1926), xx–xxi. Since Quiller-Couch refers to a scene of 'Shylock's return', not in the Shakespearian text, he has evidently been influenced by Irving's celebrated Victorian production and the tradition it established: 'So Shylock returns from a gay abhorrent banquet to knock on his empty and emptied house' (p. xx). The Variorum cites a Victorian critic who is even more sternly disapproving: 'the pert, disobedient Jessica . . . Her conduct I regard as in a high degree reprehensible; and those who have the care of families must, I think, feel as I do. She was a worthless minx . . . She selfishly forgot the duty of a daughter when she should have most remembered it' (*The Merchant of Venice*, ed. W. W. Furness (New Variorum Edition; Philadelphia: J. B. Lippincott Company, 1916), 443).

4. Graham Midgley, '*The Merchant of Venice*: A Reconsideration', in John Wilders (ed.), *Shakespeare, The Merchant of Venice: A Casebook* (London: Macmillan, 1969), 198.

5. C. L. Barber, *Shakespeare's Festive Comedy* (Princeton: Princeton University Press, 1972), 169, 180.

6. John Russell Brown, *Shakespeare and his Comedies* (London: Methuen, 1962), 70.

7. René Girard, '"To Entrap the Wisest": A Reading of *The Merchant of Venice*', in Edward W. Said (ed.), *Literature and Society* (Baltimore: Johns Hopkins University Press, 1980), 100.

8. A. D. Moody, *Shakespeare: The Merchant of Venice* (London: Edward Arnold, 1964), 10.

9. The speech is a particular favourite among critics on the alert for a dissenting or oppositional voice in *The Merchant of Venice*: see, e.g., Terry Eagleton (*William Shakespeare* (Oxford: Blackwell, 1986), 47), who interprets Shylock's lines as deconstructing Venetian law as 'class law'; Kiernan Ryan (*Shakespeare*, 3rd edn. (Basingstoke: Palgrave, 2002), 19–20); and Judith Koffler ('Terror and Mutilation in the Golden Age', *Human Rights Quarterly*, 5 (1983), 127–8). In the 1987 RSC production, Antony Sher as Shylock underlined the point by physically seizing a black attendant and displaying him to the audience: see James C. Bulman, *Shakespeare in Performance: The Merchant of Venice* (Manchester: Manchester University Press, 1991), 124–5.

10. Barber, *Shakespeare's Festive Comedy*, 118; cf. E. E. Stoll, *Shakespeare Studies* (New York: Macmillan, 1927), 312–16.

11. Brown, *Shakespeare and his Comedies*, 73; Barber, *Shakespeare's Festive Comedy*, 182.

12. Philip Brockbank, *Players of Shakespeare* (Cambridge: Cambridge University Press, 1985), 22–3.

13. Ryan, *Shakespeare*, 19.

14. Derek Cohen's reading of this speech as 'wheedling self-exculpation', which 'Shakespeare intended ... to elicit detestation for one in a privileged and powerful position who knowingly and deliberately abases himself in a plea for unmerited sympathy', seems particularly perverse ('Shakespeare and the Idea of the Jew', in his *Shakespearean Motives* (London: Macmillan, 1988), 114), though Stoll is equally confident about Shakespeare's anti-Semitic intentions (Stoll, *Shakespeare Studies*, 262–72).

15. Brockbank, *Players of Shakespeare*, 12, 19.

16. Koffler, 'Terror and Mutilation in the Golden Age', 33–4.

17. Barber, *Shakespeare's Festive Comedy*, 182.

18. Samuel Johnson, *Johnson on Shakespeare*, ed. Arthur Sherbo, in *Works*, vii (New Haven: Yale University Press, 1968), 226.

19. Girard, ' "To Entrap the Wisest" ', 115.

20. Neville Coghill, 'The Basis of Shakespearian Comedy' (1950), in *Collected Papers* (Brighton: Harvester, 1998), 278.

21. Daniel Kornstein, *Kill All the Lawyers? Shakespeare's Legal Appeal* (Princeton: Princeton University Press, 1994), 73–4; for Coke as champion of 'the inviolability of the common law's authority', see Stephen Cohen, 'The Quality of Mercy: Law, Equity and Ideology in *The Merchant of Venice*', *Mosaic*, 27/4 (Dec. 1994), 37.

22. E. F. J. Tucker, 'The Letter of the Law in *The Merchant of Venice*', *Shakespeare Survey*, 29 (1976), 94; Lawrence Danson, *The Harmonies of* The Merchant of Venice (New Haven: Yale University Press, 1978), 83–6. Tucker, writing in 1976, effectively demolishes arguments by earlier scholars that *The Merchant of Venice* explicitly or implicitly comments on jurisdictional disputes between civil and common lawyers, siding with those jurists arguing for the discretionary powers of royal prerogative (pp. 93–101). Sokol and Sokol point out that 'no equitable relief from Shylock's bond is mentioned during the trial scene or elsewhere' in the play, and that Portia does not contest Shylock's claim that 'the law regulating his bond cannot be overturned' (B.

J. and Mary Sokol, *Shakespeare's Legal Language: A Dictionary* (London: Athlone, 2000), 40, 46).

23. Danson, *The Harmonies of* The Merchant of Venice, 61, 63.
24. Hyam Maccoby, 'The Figure of Shylock', *Midstream*, 16 (Feb. 1970), 57–9.
25. Coghill, 'The Basis of Shakespearian Comedy', 280–1.
26. A position similar to Coghill's is argued in Danson,*The Harmonies of* The Merchant of Venice, 104–9; and Barbara Lewalski, 'Biblical Allusion and Allegory in *The Merchant of Venice*', *Shakespeare Quarterly*, 13 (1962), 339–42. Shapiro has a useful discussion of the theme of conversion in the play, in relation to millenarian and other tracts on conversion during this period (James Shapiro, *Shakespeare and the Jews* (New York: Columbia University Press, 1996), 130–65). Critics who find the treatment of Venetian justice in Act IV problematical include Moody, *Shakespeare*, 38–44; Koffler, 'Terror and Mutilation in the Golden Age', 129–34; and Shapiro, *Shakespeare and the Jews*, 187–9. Richard Wilson, citing Foucault, sees mercy as a stratagem of authority: the exercise of mercy 'reinforces authority even as it forswears force' (*Will Power: Essays on Shakespearean Authority* (New York: Routledge, 1993), 132).
27. Moody, *Shakespeare*, 22.
28. Kornstein, *Kill All the Lawyers?*, 69.
29. Rudolf von Ihering (1886), in *The Merchant of Venice*, ed. Furness, 410–11.
30. Moody, *Shakespeare*, 41, 43.
31. Kornstein, *Kill All the Lawyers?*, 80.
32. Patrick Stewart, in Brockbank, *Players of Shakespeare*, 27.
33. John Russell Brown, 'The Realization of Shylock: A Theatrical Criticism', in John Russell Brown and Bernard Harris (eds.), *Early Shakespeare* (Stratford-upon-Avon Studies; London: Edward Arnold, 1961), 204–5.
34. Bulman, *Shakespeare in Performance*, 95.
35. Moody, *Shakespeare*, 59.

CHAPTER 5. DISCORD AND HARMONY

1. *The Merchant of Venice*, ed. W. W. Furness (New Variorum Edition; Philadelphia: J. B. Lippincott Company, 1916), 237–8.
2. H. B. Charlton, *Shakespearian Comedy* (London: Methuen, 1938), 124, 159–60. For a similar view by a critic who sees the play as 'the tragedy of Shylock', see Walter Raleigh, *Shakespeare* (London: Macmillan, 1907), 150–1: 'The Fifth Act of *The Merchant of Venice* is an exquisite piece of romantic comedy, but it is a welcome distraction, not a full solution . . . The revengeful Jew . . . keeps possession of the play, and the memory of him gives to these beautiful closing scenes an undesigned air of heartless frivolity.'
3. Sigrid Burckhardt, '*The Merchant of Venice*: The Gentle Bond', in John Wilders (ed.), *Shakespeare, The Merchant of Venice: A Casebook* (London: Macmillan, 1969), 211–12.
4. Lawrence Danson, *The Harmonies of* The Merchant of Venice (New Haven: Yale University Press, 1978), 189; C. L. Barber, *Shakespeare's Festive Comedy* (Princeton: Princeton University Press, 1972), 187.

5. A. D. Moody, *Shakespeare: The Merchant of Venice* (London: Edward Arnold, 1964), 45, 47.
6. Barber, *Shakespeare's Festive Comedy*, 188.
7. Miriam Gilbert, *Shakespeare at Stratford: The Merchant of Venice* (London: Arden Shakespeare, 2002), 146.
8. Burckhardt, *'The Merchant of Venice*: The Gentle Bond', 221.
9. Accounts of Act V that emphasize the implicit rivalry between Portia and Antonio include Coppélia Kahn, 'The Cuckoo's Note: Male Friendship and Cuckoldry in *The Merchant of Venice*', in Peter Erickson and Coppélia Kahn (eds.), *Shakespeare's 'Rough Magic'* (Newark, Del.: University of Delaware Press, 1985), 104–7; Keith Geary, 'The Nature of Portia's Victory: Turning to Men in *The Merchant of Venice*', *Shakespeare Survey*, 37 (1984), 58–60, 63–7; and Catherine Belsey, 'Love in Venice', *Shakespeare Survey*, 44 (1991), 49–53.
10. Ibid. 47.
11. On Gratiano's lines, which end the play, see Kahn, 'The Cuckoo's Note', 109–10; Geary, 'The Nature of Portia's Victory', 66–7; and Lisa Jardine, *Reading Shakespeare Historically* (London: Routledge, 1996), 62–3. 'I'll mar the young clerk's pen', Gratiano's angry interjection, is even more explicit in its anatomical reference.
12. See Kahn, 'The Cuckoo's Note', 105–6. According to Kahn, 'from Portia's point of view, women aren't inherently fickle, as misogyny holds them to be; rather, they practice betrayal defensively, in retaliation for comparable injuries' (p. 110). For similar arguments in poems attacking the double standard by Aphra Behn, see my *Sexual Freedom in Restoration Literature* (Cambridge: Cambridge University Press, 1995), 141–7.
13. Gilbert, *Shakespeare at Stratford*, 151.
14. Geary, 'The Nature of Portia's Victory', 67.
15. Gilbert, *Shakespeare at Stratford*, 152.
16. Moody, *Shakespeare*, 56.

117

Select Bibliography

EDITIONS

The Merchant of Venice, ed. W. W. Furness (New Variorum Edition; Philadelphia: J. B. Lippincott Company, 1916).
The Merchant of Venice, ed. A. Quiller-Couch and J. Dover Wilson (Cambridge: Cambridge University Press, 1926).

The Merchant of Venice, ed. John Russell Brown (Arden Edition; London: Methuen, 1964).
The Merchant of Venice, ed. W. Moelwyn Merchant (Harmondsworth: Penguin, 1967).
The Merchant of Venice, ed. M. M. Mahood (New Cambridge Edition; Cambridge University Press, 1987).
The Merchant of Venice, ed. Jay L. Halio (Oxford: Oxford University Press, 1993).
The Riverside Shakespeare, ed. G. Blakemore Evans and J. J. M. Tobin, 2nd edn. (Boston: Houghton Mifflin, 1997).

CRITICAL STUDIES AND MISCELLANEOUS REFERENCES

Auden, W. H., *The Dyer's Hand and Other Essays* (New York: Vintage Books, 1968).
Bacon, Francis, *The Essays*, ed. John Pitcher (Harmondsworth: Penguin Books, 1985).
Baldwin, Thomas W., *The Organization and Personnel of the Shakespearean Company* (Princeton: Princeton University Press, 1927).
Barber, C. L., *Shakespeare's Festive Comedy* (Princeton: Princeton University Press, 1972).
Barton, John, *Playing Shakespeare* (London: Methuen, 1984).
Belsey, Catherine, 'Disrupting Sexual Difference: Meaning and Gender in the Comedies', in John Drakakis (ed.), *Alternative Shakespeares* (London: Routledge, 1988).

—— 'Love in Venice', *Shakespeare Survey*, 44 (1991), 41–53.

Boose, Lynda, 'The Father and the Bride in Shakespeare', *PMLA* 97 (1982), 325–47.

Brockbank, Philip, *Players of Shakespeare* (Cambridge: Cambridge University Press, 1985).

Brown, John Russell, 'The Realization of Shylock: A Theatrical Criticism', in John Russell Brown and Bernard Harris (eds.), *Early Shakespeare* (Stratford-upon Avon Studies; London: Edward Arnold, 1961), 186–209.

—— *Shakespeare and his Comedies* (London: Methuen, 1962).

Bulman, James C., *Shakespeare in Performance: The Merchant of Venice* (Manchester: Manchester University Press, 1991).

Bulman, James C. and Coursen, H. C. (eds.), *Shakespeare on Television* (Hanover, NH: University Press of New England, 1988).

Burckhardt, Sigurd, '*The Merchant of Venice*: The Gentle Bond', in John Wilders (ed.), *Shakespeare,* The Merchant of Venice*: A Casebook* (London: Macmillan, 1969), 208–23.

Chambers, David, and Pullan, Brian (eds.), *Venice: A Documentary History, 1450–1630* (Oxford: Blackwell, 1993).

Charlton, H. B., *Shakespearian Comedy* (London: Methuen, 1938).

Chernaik, Warren, *Sexual Freedom in Restoration Literature* (Cambridge: Cambridge University Press, 1995).

Coghill, Neville, 'The Basis of Shakespearian Comedy' (1950), in *Collected Papers* (Brighton: Harvester, 1998).

Cohen, Derek, 'Shakespeare and the Idea of the Jew', in his *Shakespearean Motives* (London: Macmillan, 1988), 104–18.

Cohen, Stephen, 'The Quality of Mercy: Law, Equity and Ideology in *The Merchant of Venice*', *Mosaic*, 27/4 (Dec. 1994), 37.

Cohen, Walter, '*The Merchant of Venice* and the Possibilities of Historical Criticism', *ELH* 49 (1982), 765–89.

Contarini, Gaspare, *The Commonwealth and Government of Venice*, trans. Lewis Lewkenor (1599), facsimile reprint (Amsterdam: Da Capo Press, 1969).

Cook, Judith, *Shakespeare's Players* (London: Harrap, 1983).

Danson, Lawrence, *The Harmonies of* The Merchant of Venice (New Haven: Yale University Press, 1978).

Draper, John W., 'Usury in *The Merchant of Venice*', *Modern Philology*, 33 (1935), 37–47.

Eagleton, Terry, *William Shakespeare* (Oxford: Blackwell, 1986).

Edelman, Charles, 'Which is the Jew that Shakespeare Knew?: Shylock on the Elizabethan Stage', *Shakespeare Survey*, 52 (1999), 99–106.

Engle, Lars, ' "Thrift is Blessing": Exchange and Explanation in *The Merchant of Venice*', *Shakespeare Quarterly*, 37 (1986), 20–37.

Fiedler, Leslie, *The Stranger in Shakespeare* (New York: Stein & Day, 1972).

Fink, Zera S., *The Classical Republicans* (Evanston, Ill.: Northwestern University Press, 1945).

Finlay, Robert, *Politics in Renaissance Venice* (London: Ernest Benn, 1980).

Frye, Northrop, 'The Argument of Comedy', in *English Institute Essays, 1948* (New York: Columbia University Press, 1949).

—— *An Anatomy of Criticism* (Princeton: Princeton University Press, 1957).

Geary, Keith, 'The Nature of Portia's Victory: Turning to Men in *The Merchant of Venice*', *Shakespeare Survey*, 37 (1984), 44–68.

Gilbert, Miriam, *Shakespeare at Stratford: The Merchant of Venice* (London: Arden Shakespeare, 2002).

Gillies, John, *Shakespeare and the Geography of Difference* (Cambridge: Cambridge University Press, 1994).

Girard, René, ' "To Entrap the Wisest": A Reading of *The Merchant of Venice*', in Edward W. Said (ed.), *Literature and Society* (Baltimore: Johns Hopkins University Press, 1980), 100–19.

Granville, George, Lord Lansdowne, *The Jew of Venice* (London, 1701; repr. London: Haymarket Press, 1969).

Greenblatt, Stephen, *Shakespearean Negotiations* (Oxford: Clarendon Press, 1988).

Gross, John, *Shylock: Four Hundred Years in the Life of a Legend* (London: Vintage, 1994).

Highfill, Philip H., et al., *A Biographical Dictionary of Actors, Actresses . . . and Other Stage Personnel in London, 1660-1800*, 16 vols. (Carbondale and Edwardsville, Ill.: Southern Illinois University Press, 1973–93).

Howard, Jean E., 'Crossdressing, the Theatre, and Gender Struggle in Early Modern England', *Shakespeare Quarterly*, 39 (1988), 418–40.

Hughes, Alan, *Henry Irving, Shakespearean* (Cambridge: Cambridge University Press, 1981).

Jardine, Lisa, *Still Harping on Daughters* (London: Harvester, 1989).

—— *Reading Shakespeare Historically* (London: Routledge, 1996).

Johnson, Samuel, *Johnson on Shakespeare*, ed. Arthur Sherbo, in *Works*, vii (New Haven: Yale University Press, 1968).

Kahn, Coppélia, 'The Cuckoo's Note: Male Friendship and Cuckoldry in *The Merchant of Venice*', in Peter Erickson and Coppélia Kahn (eds.), *Shakespeare's 'Rough Magic'* (Newark, Del.: University of Delaware Press, 1985), 104–12.

Katukani, Michiko, 'Debate over Shylock Simmers once again', *New York Times*, 22 Feb. 1981, section 2, pp. 1, 30.

Koffler, Judith, 'Terror and Mutilation in the Golden Age', *Human Rights Quarterly*, 5 (1983), 116–34.

Kornstein, Daniel, *Kill All the Lawyers? Shakespeare's Legal Appeal* (Princeton: Princeton University Press, 1994), 65–89.

Lelyveld, Toby, *Shylock on the Stage* (London: Routledge & Kegan Paul, 1961).

Lewalski, Barbara, 'Biblical Allusion and Allegory in *The Merchant of Venice*', *Shakespeare Quarterly*, 13 (1962), 321–43.

Maccoby, Hyam, 'The Figure of Shylock', *Midstream*, 16 (Feb. 1970), 56–69.

Midgley, Graham, '*The Merchant of Venice*: A Reconsideration', in John Wilders (ed.), *Shakespeare, The Merchant of Venice: A Casebook* (London: Macmillan, 1969), 193–207.

Miller, Jonathan, *Subsequent Performances* (London: Faber & Faber, 1986).

Moody, A. D., *Shakespeare: The Merchant of Venice* (London: Edward Arnold, 1964).

Nelson, Benjamin, *The Idea of Usury*, 2nd edn. (Chicago: University of Chicago Press, 1969).

Nevo, Ruth, *Comic Transformations in Shakespeare* (London: Methuen, 1980).

Newman, Karen, 'Portia's Ring: Unruly Women and Structures of Exchange in *The Merchant of Venice'*, *Shakespeare Quarterly*, 38 (1987), 19–33.

Olivier, Laurence, *On Acting* (London: Sceptre, 1987).

Orgel, Stephen, *Impersonations* (Cambridge: Cambridge University Press, 1996).

Overton, Bill, *The Merchant of Venice: Text and Performance* (Basingstoke: Macmillan, 1987).

Park, Clara Claiborne, 'As We Like It: How a Girl can be Smart and still Popular', in Carol Lenz, Gayle Greene, and Carol Neely (eds.), *The Woman's Part: Feminist Criticism of Shakespeare* (Urbana, Ill.: University of Illinois Press, 1983).

Pullan, Brian, *Rich and Poor in Renaissance Venice* (Oxford: Blackwell, 1971).

—— *The Jews of Europe and the Inquisition of Venice, 1550–1670* (Oxford: Blackwell, 1983).

Raleigh, Walter, *Shakespeare* (London: Macmillan, 1907).

Ryan, Kiernan, *Shakespeare*, 3rd edn. (Basingstoke: Palgrave, 2002).

Sartre, Jean-Paul, *Anti-Semite and Jew*, trans. George J. Becker (New York: Schocken Books, 1948).

Shapiro, James, *Shakespeare and the Jews* (New York: Columbia University Press, 1996).

Shaw, Bernard, *Our Theatres in the Nineties*, 3 vols. (London: Constable, 1948).

Sokol, B. J., and Sokol, Mary, *Shakespeare's Legal Language: A Dictionary* (London: Athlone, 2000).

Stoll, E. E., *Shakespeare Studies* (New York: Macmillan, 1927).

Tucker, E. F. J., 'The Letter of the Law in *The Merchant of Venice'*, *Shakespeare Survey*, 29 (1976), 93–101.

Verch, Maria, '*The Merchant of Venice* on the German Stage since 1945', *Theatre History Studies*, 5 (1985), 84–94.

Wesker, Arnold, *Shylock and Other Plays* (London: Penguin, 1990).

Wilders, John (ed.), *Shakespeare,* The Merchant of Venice*: A Casebook* (London: Macmillan, 1969).

Wilson, Richard, *Will Power: Essays on Shakespearean Authority* (New York: Routledge, 1993), 126–68.

Wilson, Thomas, *A Discourse upon Usury* (1572), ed. R. H. Tawney (London: G. Bell & Sons, 1925).

Index